MW01236221

TRUTHS FOR KINGDOM LIVING

Fifty-Two Inspirational Truths
and Other Helps

By
Ruby Taylor Ridgill and
Francine Taylor Morton

Bloomington, IN   Milton Keynes, UK

authorHOUSE™

AuthorHouse™
1663 Liberty Drive, Suite 200
Bloomington, IN 47403
www.authorhouse.com
Phone: 1-800-839-8640

AuthorHouse™ UK Ltd.
500 Avebury Boulevard
Central Milton Keynes, MK9 2BE
www.authorhouse.co.uk
Phone: 08001974150

© 2006 Ruby Taylor Ridgill and Francine Taylor Morton. All rights reserved.
P.O. Box 292, Alcolu, South Carolina, Facsimile: 954-748-3453
KingdomLivingToday@Yahoo.com

No part of this book may be reproduced, stored in
a retrieval system, or transmitted by any means
without the written permission of the author.

All scripture quotations taken from the authorized
King James Version of the Holy Bible.

First published by AuthorHouse 3/6/2006

ISBN: 1-4259-1078-5 (sc)

Printed in the United States of America
Bloomington, Indiana

This book is printed on acid-free paper.

Dedication

To Our HEAVENLY FATHER,

Our wonderful and magnificent Friend, this book is **Yours**. Thank You for entrusting Your truth to us, Your daughters. This favor is not because we are worthy of honor, but because we are willing to honor You.

You gave us new hearts and charged us to bring, with clarity and simplicity, Your word to Your people. May we never fail You, forsake You or leave You is our humble prayer.

And
To Our Daughters,

Beautiful, talented, and chosen, Rev. Lori Morton, Rev. Alice Ridgill and Aleanna Morton, we love you dearly. You are our *sisters in the faith* and you bring us great joy.

We pass on to you the love and legacy from our mother, ***And all nations shall call you blessed: for ye shall be a delightsome land, saith the Lord of hosts.*** *Malachi 3:12.* May our lives always be the Godly examples you wish to emulate is our earnest desire.

Inspiration

As you begin your journey through this book, let us share with you how it came to be.

We can remember many wonderful life lessons and life experiences over the past years. One stands out as "life changing" to the extent that it is indelibly imprinted into our minds, our hearts, and our lives.

A new heart will I give you– a new Spirit will I put within you, rings clearly to us each day. This promise of God in Ezekiel 36:26,27 truly became ours three years ago in an experience above and beyond anything we could have imagined. It sealed a wavering Christian walk and bonded two sisters to daily prayer, a lifestyle that continues today.

Our prayer chamber is fully and completely shared with the Holy Spirit. We never come away from this chamber without having had an encounter with the King.

The precious "truths" in this book were *personally* and *privately* deposited in us over several years by Him, who lives in us. These "truths" are validated, under girded and reinforced by Holy Spirit inspired scriptures from the Bible. They are commanded out of us and into print, by that same Spirit for the divine purpose of making a deposit into your spirit.

Our prayer is that you will trust in the sacred truth of God's word and be inspired to seek "life-changing" experiences. May you always invite Him into your prayer chamber as you daily seek to live victoriously in His Kingdom.

The Authors

Table of Contents

Acknowledgments

*T*o the memory of our departed parents, David and Alice Taylor, who were patient, kind and loving and whose effectual prayers continue to cover their children today.

To John Haynesworth, my best friend, thank you. To Charles Morton, my husband and best friend, thank you. We are so very blessed that you bring an element of calm resolve into our lives. Your kindness and understanding are invaluable.

To our sister, Minnie Taylor Hudson, you are a source of strength. Thank you for inspiring and challenging us in our Christian walk.

To our *Kingdom children*, Mitchell and Mary Adger, Isiwe Cooke, Lisa Coker, Shavan Fulton, Cathy Kennedy, John and Janice Nelson, Gregory Taylor and Tela Witherspoon, we are grateful that you allow us to share in your lives. We grant to you our prayer that the glory of God rests upon you and you walk therein all the days of your lives.

To our *Kingdom friends,* Mother Hattie Courley, Dr. Robert and Corine Bligen, Dr. Mack King Carter, Pastor Charles Foxe, Shirley Rose Howard, Willie and Jennifer Howard, Rev. L.G. Mathis, Callie Melton, Pastor C.J. McBride, Youlanda Thomas, Rev. Constance Walker, Evangelist Angela Williams and Rev. George P. Windley, we salute you. Your prayers, teaching, leadership and strength are fundamental to our Christian experience. We have leaned on your shoulders and we have tested your patience. You have proven faithful time and time again. Where would we be without you? Your encouragement and your precious gift of friendship are appreciated.

To Mrs. Willie F. Morton, thank you for applying your editing skills to this work.

To our niece, Cynthia Taylor, thank you for applying your journalistic skills to this work.

Many other lives (you know who you are) have touched ours and many are the remembrances and occurrences of love and joy shared. You are special to us and you know that we are grateful to you. Thank you for helping to make this book a reality. Finally, our part of this Kingdom assignment is complete!

Forward

*D*evotional time with God is priceless. Of all the things that we may give to God (our money, talent, etc.), there is nothing that He wants more than our time. What God wants from us is a relationship.

A relationship is not built on an isolated encounter, but rather it must be established in intimacy by spending time together day after day. To have the relationship with Christ in the way that He so desires, we must spend time in his presence. It must be more than the few precious moments we shared when we asked him to be our personal savior and He received us into his Kingdom.

Truths for Kingdom Living is an awesome tool for building a relationship with Christ. It gives us Bible-based truths, supports us in our prayer life, and helps us hide the word of God in our hearts with scripture readings. It is destined to bring increase into our lives – spiritually, emotionally and physically. It will impact our lives in a powerful way and build our confidence in a faithful God.

Indeed, there are various inspirational books for our reading, but this one is a must and should be read daily. May you be blessed as you grow in your relationship with our Heavenly Father.

Derrick Fort, Senior Pastor
Great Commission Ministries
Lake City and Manning, SC

Preface

We were all born in sin and shaped in iniquity. Before we accepted Jesus as Savior and Lord, our lives were self-directed. All that we thought, said, did, saw, or felt was based on past experiences and current circumstances. We diligently promoted the "self life", usually at the expense of disrupting the lives of others. Love, or what we erroneously termed as love, was totally reserved for self and others who were deemed worthy. Those who conformed to our schemes and devices fit into our lives and our plans.

Such was the essence of our existence. It's who we were. Our unspoken motto was some variation of a get even or get ahead tactic. After all, without fail, self had to prevail. Everytime! Everywhere!

The Apostle Paul enlightens us in Titus 3:3: *For we ourselves also were sometimes foolish, disobedient, deceived, serving divers lusts and pleasures, living in malice and envy, hateful, and hating one another.*

We were not created to live that way. Deep inside, we yearned for change, but there was always a void. Life was empty. Little did we know that only God could fill the emptiness and make us whole.

Paul continues to enlighten us in Titus 3:4-7: *But after that the kindness and love of God our Savior toward man appeared, Not by works of righteousness which we have done, but according to his mercy he saved us, by the washing of regeneration, and renewing of the Holy Ghost; Which he shed on us abundantly through Jesus Christ our Savior; That being justified by his grace, we should be made heirs according to the hope of eternal life.*

We have need of a new life and self-rule needs to be abolished. Our yearning is to be citizens of the Kingdom system where Christ rules supreme in splendor and royalty. It is here that we can experience the God-kind of life. It is here that we can be filled.

In this Kingdom, we are not only Christ's constituents and subjects; He calls us friend. We are bound to loyalty and service under His authority and in His system of governments. This is the Kingdom of God and this system is within us. The Spirit of God indwells all in this Kingdom and guides us into all truth. The truth of God, which is the will of God, is also the wisdom and word of God. The word provides the reality of provision for the children of the King.

Kingdom living is a confirmed lifestyle of loyal citizens and a royal King in the faithful establishment, secure bond, and constant fellowship of an eternal **word** centered relationship.

I Peter 2:9 records, *But ye are a chosen generation, a royal priesthood, an holy nation, a peculiar people; that ye should shew forth the praises of him who hath called you out of darkness into his marvellous light.*

Although we are in the world, we are not of the world. Our loyalty is to Royalty. Royalty speaks a spiritual language. His language is the word of God. It is the official language of the Kingdom. Loyalty hears this language. Loyalty then willingly and obediently follows the commands and decrees of Royalty, both from a legal written document and from spoken edicts. This is our act of faith. This pleases Royalty. Royalty sees both the new heart and the holy life and rewards Loyalty with the abundant life made sure by the presence of the King.

If you are not Loyalty, become so! Live in the pages of this book and in the word of God. Recognize your place and your picture in the portrait of the Kingdom family. All of God's children are there. He makes us royalty (kings and priests) in His Kingdom.

The born-again, spirit-filled, spirit-led life is **absolutely real and absolutely authentic. Everything else is an** empty copy or counterfeit. **The spirit in** us is our connection to the Spirit of Christ. Bonded together and living in His righteousness, we share the very same domain--THE KINGDOM of GOD -- where Christ is King!

BUT
SEEK YE FIRST
THE KINGDOM
OF GOD,
AND HIS
RIGHTEOUSNESS;
AND ALL
THESE THINGS
SHALL BE ADDED
UNTO YOU.

MATTHEW 6:33

◇◇◇◇◇◇◇◇

PART I
SALVIFIC HELPS

Hope, preparation
and expectation for
Kingdom living

Introduction to Salvific Helps

*T*he God of the Universe is calling His creation to Himself through the ministry of the Holy Spirit in the earth today. The unsaved is being called to salvation, the backslider is being called to restoration, and the true believer is being called to holiness. Our service to the Father is one of giving ourselves [which is all that we have to give] in worship to Him. We are His. Our very breath belongs to Him. So we ask ourselves this question: Do we have the right to rob Him of that which belongs to Him by natural/physical creation and that which also belongs to Him through the redeeming blood of Jesus Christ? The answer-no!!

The yielded life, as promised in the Bible, is one of victory in Christ. No longer should we relent to the overbearing, overpowering evil of satan. He hates God. Would he not also hate us? We can and must resist the devil. As children of God, born into His Kingdom, we can render satan's works against us ineffective. We have this authority in the name of Jesus.

The salvific helps which follow will guide us through scriptures that convince the unyielded soul to come into allegiance to the King of Glory --- the Lord God Almighty.

Pathway to Repentance

*I*n the book of Jeremiah, we get insights concerning the fallen nature of mankind and the absolute hopelessness of this natural state. Only He who created us can change this state and it **must be changed** if we are to claim Christ as King.

The heart is deceitful above all things, and desperately wicked: who can know it? I the Lord search the heart, I try the reins, even to give every man according to his ways, and according to the fruit of his doings.

Jeremiah 17:9,10

Then I went down to the potter's house, and, behold, he wrought a work on the wheels. And the vessel that he made of clay was marred in the hand of the potter: so he made it again another vessel, as seemed good to the potter to make it.

Jeremiah 18:3,4

In Psalm 51:1-3, King David lamented his sinful state and prayed for the mercy of God to purge and deliver him. In our identification with the Psalmist, we too hear our hearts crying: *Have mercy upon me, O God, according to thy loving kindness: according unto the multitude of thy tender mercies blot out my transgressions. Wash me throughly from mine iniquity, and cleanse me from my sin. For I acknowledge my transgressions: and my sin is ever before me.*

The Bible tells us that the blood of Jesus has been appropriated for the remission of sin. The finished work at Calvary belongs to us. The veil that prevented us from approaching the throne room of God has been removed. Once we were called aliens and strangers from the covenants of promise. Now the shed blood of Christ makes us near. We can boldly enter the presence of God to obtain mercy and grace.

That at that time ye were without Christ, being aliens from the commonwealth of Israel, and strangers from the covenants of promise, having no hope and without God in the world: But now in Christ Jesus ye who sometimes were far off are made nigh by the blood of Christ. For he is our peace, who hath made both one, and hath broken down the middle wall of partition between us; And came and preached peace to you which were afar off, and to them that were nigh. For through him we both have access by one Spirit unto the Father. Now therefore ye are no more strangers and foreigners, but fellow-citizens with the saints, and of the household of God;
Ephesians 2:12-14; 17-19

Let us therefore come boldly unto the throne of grace, that we may obtain mercy, and find grace to help in time of need.
Hebrews 4:16

Scriptural Call to Repentance and Salvation

*I*n the innermost part of humanity, there is a deep longing - an empty place yearning to be filled. The desire for the things offered by the world system always proves to be fruitless. Unless and until we heed the promptings of the Spirit of God, we simply keep on searching and never finding; knocking, but never able to enter.

God does not give up on us in our *lostness*. He seeks the lost to bring to a place of willingness to repent. One must intentionally and deliberately confess and desire to turn away from sin. One must die to self and be born of the Spirit. First, deny self the right to rule in life from a natural/carnal advantage. Secondly, allow Christ the authority to rule in life from a spiritual advantage.

God gave Jesus as a spotless lamb to atone for our sins and redeem us from the curse brought on by Adam's **disobedience** in the Garden of Eden. He gives the Holy Spirit to summon His created beings to yield to the authority and rulership brought on by Jesus' **obedience** in the Garden of Gethsemane.

Jesus accepted death, thereby saying to the Father, *not My will, but Thine be done*. Because of His faithfulness in laying down His life, we can be free from the law of sin and death. On the other hand, Adam partook of the forbidden fruit, thereby saying to the Father, *not Your will, but mine be done.* He plunged himself and all mankind lodged within him into spiritual death.

It is our Father's desire that we reign as kings and priests, giving glory to Him and abiding in His

Kingdom. The scripture tells us in Luke 12:32b, *...for it is your Father's good pleasure to give you the kingdom.* He seeks committed souls to be vessels of honor in the earth. He grants us the privilege to have Him live in us and through us. We are one with Him and in Him we have our being. We become the abiding place for the Holy One.

The following verses echo loudly and clearly the call of the Holy Spirit for God's created beings to be delivered from the bondage of corruption. He calls us to come into manifestation as the sons and daughters of God. The sons and daughters who are heirs of God and joint heirs with Jesus Christ - adopted into His Holy Family:

The Lord is not slack concerning his promise, as some men count slackness; but is longsuffering to us-ward, not willing that any should perish, but that all should come to repentance.

II Peter 3:9

Jesus answered, Verily, verily, I say unto thee, Except a man be born of water and of the Spirit, he cannot enter into the kingdom of God. That which is born of the flesh is flesh; and that which is born of the Spirit is spirit. Marvel not that I said unto thee, Ye must be born again.

John 3:5-7

This is a faithful saying, and worthy of all acceptation, that Christ Jesus came into the world to save sinners; of whom I am chief.

I Timothy 1:15

And she shall bring forth a son, and thou shalt call his name JESUS: for he shall save his people from their sins.

Matthew 1:21

For God so loved the world, that he gave his only begotten Son, that whosoever believeth in him should not perish, but have everlasting life. For God sent not his Son into the world to condemn the world; but that the world through him might be saved.

John 3:16,17

For the Son of man is come to save that which was lost.

Matthew 18:11

Even when we were dead in sins, hath quickened us together with Christ, (by grace ye are saved;) And hath raised us up together, and made us sit together in heavenly places in Christ Jesus: That in the ages to come he might shew the exceeding riches of his grace in his kindness toward us through Christ Jesus. For by grace are ye saved through faith; and that not of yourselves: it is the gift of God: Not of works, lest any man should boast. For we are his workmanship, created in Christ Jesus unto good works, which God hath before ordained that we should walk in them.

Ephesians 2:5-10

If thou shall confess with thy mouth the Lord Jesus, and shalt believe in thine heart that God hath raised him from the dead thou shalt be saved. For with the heart man believeth unto righteousness; and with the mouth confession is made unto salvation. For the scripture saith, Whosoever believeth on him shall not be ashamed.

Romans 10:9-11

And in that day thou shalt say, O Lord, I will praise thee: though thou wast angry with me, thine anger is turned away and thou comfortedst me. Behold, God is my salvation; I will trust, and not be afraid: for the Lord JEHOVAH is my strength and my song; he also is become my salvation. Therefore with joy shall ye draw water out of the wells of salvation.

Isaiah 12:1-3

Prayer for Salvation

We all are given the freedom to decide our 'spirit' destiny. Although we are born in sin and shaped in iniquity, Jesus gave His life at Calvary that we might have forgiveness of sin. We can be changed from the *darkness* of sin to the *light* of life. This *change* is the salvific experience. In His conversation with Nicodemus in John 3:3, Jesus calls it *born again*. It is not a process and does not require an extended period of time for fruition. One simply makes a decision in the heart and breathes it to the Savior. All else is His work.

> *Let not sin therefore reign in your mortal body, that ye should obey it in the lusts thereof.*
>
> Romans 6:12

The Apostle Paul offers us help in making a 'Kingdom choice' in Romans 6:23. *For the wages of sin is death; but the gift of God is eternal life through Jesus Christ our Lord.*

> *I call heaven and earth to record this day against you, that I have set before you life and death, blessing and cursing, therefore choose life, that both thou and thy seed may live:*
>
> Deuteronomy 30:19

We can choose to ask Jesus to receive us into His family and into the Kingdom. We can choose to allow Him to be our Lord and King and have complete rule in and authority over our lives. We can choose to commit ourselves totally to Him. We can choose to learn and obey His word. We can choose to have a life of victory.

The choice is yours. Shall we pray?

Dear Jesus, I believe that You truly are the risen Savior. Forgive me for the sins and wrongs of my past. I have fallen short of Your glory; but now I am ready and willing to turn from darkness to light – from cursing to blessing - from death to life. I cannot change myself by my thoughts, desires or deeds. I reach forth for Your free gift of eternal life which is so graciously offered to me. I now humbly yield myself totally, entirely, and completely to You. Through my faith, which truly is Yours, I seek salvation by Your grace. Thank You for accepting me into Your Kingdom. Come into my life and live Your life through me. Amen.

Scriptural Benefits of Salvation

*P*ersons applying for an employment relationship in the world system will often inquire about the benefits associated with the position. The benefits package is received concurrent with and is supplemental to the remuneration. Often, job acceptance is based on the value and appeal of the benefits.

Persons receiving the salvific experience in the Kingdom are endowed with the lucrative benefits package God has for His children. Here are a few of the King's benefits which have great value and appeal.

Come unto me, all ye that labour and are heavy laden, and I will give you rest. Take my yoke upon you, and learn of me; for I am meek and lowly in heart: and ye shall find rest unto your souls. For my yoke is easy, and my burden is light.

Matthew 11:28-30

Call unto me, and I will answer thee, and shew thee great and mighty things, which thou knowest not.

Jeremiah 33:3

Bless the Lord, O my soul, and forget not all his benefits: Who forgiveth all thine iniquities; who healeth all thy diseases; Who redeemeth thy life from destruction; who crowneth thee with lovingkindness and tender mercies; Who satisfieth thy mouth with good things; so that thy youth is renewed like the eagle's. The Lord executeth righteousness and judgment for all that are oppressed.

Psalm 103:2-6

Blessed be the Lord, who daily loadeth us with benefits, even the God of our salvation. Selah.

Psalm 68:19

He hath not dealt with us after our sins; nor rewarded us according to our iniquities. For as the heaven is high above the earth, so great is his mercy toward them that fear him. As far as the east is from the west, so far hath he removed our transgressions from us. The Lord hath prepared his throne in the heavens; and his kingdom ruleth over all.

Psalm 103:10-12, 19

Prayer of Commitment

This prayer of commitment is included to prepare you to move into the fifty-two Truths that follow. It will allow you to reflect on *who* you are, *where* you are, and *what* you will do to impact the outcome of your existence in the earth and your life in the Kingdom of God.

Make this prayer your very own.

Our Father, You tell us to pray without ceasing. Therefore, in obedience to Your Word, I come in the name of my Lord and Savior Jesus the Christ. I choose now to begin a daily prayer journey and commit my life to travel this journey with diligence.

I consider my body and say – let there be a crucifying of this carnal nature with its propensity towards selfishness and pride. In this flesh, there is no good thing. Let its deeds be mortified. I offer my body a living sacrifice, wholly, totally, and completely to You, which is my reasonable service of worship and honor. All I have to give to You is all of me. Therefore, I purpose in my heart to do – to say-to be- in this body, this earthen vessel, those things which please You.

I consider my mind and say – let there be a renewing of this mind with its propensity towards mistrust and unbelief. Let it perceive and receive the truth of Your word and Your will. I purpose in my heart to listen with my mind, using spiritual ears to hear always those things You say by Your Spirit and through Your written Word. My mind is renewed and I now have the mind of Christ. Your wisdom is formed within me.

I consider my spirit and say – let there be a releasing from the wretchedness of a fallen nature with its propensity towards sin and evil. Let the sin nature and heart of stone be removed from me and a new heart and a new spirit be grafted in. With clean hands and a pure heart I will worship You, O my God. I will ever love You with all of my heart, mind and strength.

I thank You my Father, for Christ the risen Savior and anointed King of Glory who rules and reigns supreme <u>in me</u>. I thank You for Jesus my Lord and Savior who ever makes intercession <u>for me</u> at Your right hand. I thank You for Your Holy Spirit, my Comforter and Guide, who is ever present <u>with me</u>. I thank You for the Angels of heaven which are ascending and descending, ministering <u>to me,</u> an heir of salvation. I thank You for the brilliance of Your glory as it shines <u>through me</u>. In You I live. In You I move. In You I have an abundant life.

May the abundant life of love which I shall live forever in Christ always exalt and honor You, Abba, Father. For Yours is the kingdom, for Yours is the power, for Yours is the glory, forever more. Amen.

THEY ARE NOT OF
THE WORLD, EVEN AS
I AM
NOT OF THE WORLD.
SANCTIFY THEM
THROUGH THY
TRUTH:
THY WORD IS TRUTH.
AS THOU HAST SENT
ME INTO THE WORLD,
EVEN SO HAVE I ALSO
SENT THEM
INTO THE WORLD.
AND FOR THEIR SAKES
I SANCTIFY MYSELF,
THAT THEY ALSO
MIGHT BE SANCTIFIED
THROUGH THE
TRUTH.

JOHN 17:16-19

◇◇◇◇◇◇◇◇

PART II
INSPIRATIONAL
TRUTHS

*Encouragement and
development in
Kingdom living*

Introduction to Inspirational Truths

*T*he Rhema word is often personal to the hearer and is fully backed by the written word of God. We each hear with different physical ears and with different spiritual ears. What we listen for is what we need or desire for our lives. The wealthy are not looking for a word of deliverance from a state of poverty! They have no need of it. The healed are not looking for a word of deliverance from sickness! They have no need of it. But, we all are looking for a word of victory in every arena that is adversely impacting us as individuals.

The word of God lets us know in Psalm 138:8a, *The Lord will perfect that which concerneth me.* When the Holy Spirit gives us a Rhema word from the heart of the Father, it is as real as the air we breathe. Just like that air, we must receive the word without question or hesitation. To do so, in both instances, means life. To refuse? Well…

Intimacy with the Father through the person of the Spirit is an un-common bond and a super-natural fellowship. This closeness with Him makes a life of peace and joy in a place that can worthily be described as the Father's bosom – near to His heart.

How would you respond to this scenario? What if you were worshipping and praying and while doing so, God just picked you up in His arms and allowed you to become meshed into *oneness* with Him. In His bosom? You in God and God in you? Would not that be the safest place in the universe? Surely it would! That is the place of Kingdom living. It is where the truth of God prevails. It is that place already provided for us through and in Christ Jesus.

And for their sakes I sanctify myself, that they also might be sanctified through the truth. Neither pray I for these alone, but for them also which shall believe on me through their word; That they all may be one; as thou, Father, art in me, and I in thee, that they also may be in us: that the world may believe that thou has sent me. And the glory which thou gavest me I have given them; that they may be one, even as we are one: I in them, and thou in me, that they may be made perfect in one; and that the world may know that thou hast sent me, and hast loved them, as thou has loved me. Father, I will that they also, whom thou has given me, be with me where I am; that they may behold my glory, which thou has given me:

John 17:19-24a

Join this Holy team. Those on the team are God our Father, Jesus our Savior, Christ our King, the Holy Spirit our Comforter, and the angels who ascend and descend in ministry for us. **Join Them!**

Hear the voice of the Father. Enjoy the salvation from Jesus. Abide in the Kingdom of Christ. Be guided by the Holy Spirit. Give the angels a God word to hear and minister. **Join Them!**

And it shall come to pass, if thou shalt hearken diligently unto the voice of the Lord thy God, to observe and to do all his commandments which I command thee this day, that the Lord thy God will set thee on high above all nations of the earth: And the Lord shall make thee the head, and not the tail; and thou shalt be above only, and thou shalt not be beneath; if that thou hearken unto the commandments of the Lord thy God, which I command thee this day, to observe and to do them:

Deuteronomy 28:1,13

My sheep hear my voice, and I know them, and they follow me: And I give unto them eternal life; and they shall never perish, neither shall any man pluck them out of my hand.

John 10:27,28

Names of Truths

Live A New Life

Come Unto Me

Hear My Voice

Live In Unity

Give Me Control

Pray For Leaders

Speak Creatively

Seek My Kingdom

You Are My Child

Pray

Offer Praise And Worship

Love As I Love

Celebrate Life

Repent And Obey

Stay On Course

Yield To My Spirit

Abide In Me

Die To Self

Trust Me

You Are An Overcomer

My Power Channel

Victory

You Choose

My Gifts - Salvation

I Am Your Victory

Reap In Joy

Come And Receive

My Word Will Endure

Stand

Expect The Best

Magnify Me

Shine

Set My Agenda

Live The Resurrected Life

Give

Your Prayers Are Answered

Focus On Jesus

Bear Fruit

Speak My Word

Stay In Me

Know That I Am God

Do Not Murmur

Rest In Me

Fear Not

Open The Door Of Faith

Live Holy

You Are Mine

You Are My Temple

You Are Not Alone

Forgive And Be Free

Live By Faith

Guard Your Mouth

Truth One

LIVE A NEW LIFE

The Truth

I have delivered you from death to life. You are a new creature in Me. The old is passed away and the new has come. You are My righteousness in Christ Jesus. Walk in a new direction. Think new thoughts. Speak new words. Do new deeds. Bear new fruit. Sing a new song. Live a new life!

The Scriptures

AND you hath he quickened, who were dead in trespasses and sins;

Wherein in time past ye walked according to the course of this world, according to the prince of the power of the air, the spirit that now worketh in the children of disobedience:

Ephesians 2:1,2

For he hath made him to be sin for us, who knew no sin; that we might be made the righteousness of God in him.

II Corinthians 5:21

Among whom also we all had our conversation in times past in the lusts of our flesh, fulfilling the desires of the flesh and of the mind; and were by nature the children of wrath, even as others.

But God, who is rich in mercy, for his great love wherewith he loved us,

Even when we were dead in sins, hath quickened us together with Christ, (by grace ye are saved;)

And hath raised us up together, and made us sit together in heavenly places in Christ Jesus:

That in the ages to come he might shew the exceeding riches of his grace in his kindness toward us through Christ Jesus.

Ephesians 2:3-7

Therefore if any man be in Christ, he is a new creature: old things are passed away; behold, all things are become new.

II Corinthians 5:17

Let him that stole steal no more: but rather let him labour, working with his hands the thing which is good, that he may have to give to him that needeth.

Ephesians 4:28

Brethren, I count not myself to have apprehended: but this one thing I do, forgetting those things which are behind, and reaching forth unto those things which are before,

I press toward the mark for the prize of the high calling of God in Christ Jesus.

Philippians 3:13,14

Finally, brethren, whatsoever things are true, whatsoever things are honest, whatsoever things are just, whatsoever things are pure, whatsoever things are lovely, whatsoever things are of good report; if there be any virtue, and if there be any praise, think on these things.

Philippians 4:8

...that like as Christ was raised up from the dead by the glory of the Father, even so we also should walk in newness of life.

Romans 6:4b

The Prayer

Oh Father, how very grateful I am that You have made me new. Thank You for empowering me to leave my past and live a new life. I turn away from darkness and purpose to stay in the Light – looking unto Jesus, the author and finisher of my faith.

My faith says I am anchored in Your word; therefore, by Your Spirit, I study to show myself approved unto You. My faith says strait is the gate and narrow is the way of my new life; therefore, by Your Spirit I purpose to stay on course – not straying to the right or to the left. My faith says Your thoughts are higher than mine and so are Your ways; therefore, by Your Spirit I renew my mind with Your truth and do always those things which please You. Use me for Your purpose and Your glory. Amen.

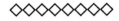

Truth Two

COME UNTO ME

The Truth

There is a place for you in Me. Come unto Me. Take My yoke upon you. For as long as we are yoked together, we agree. My yoke is easy and My burden is light. My yoke will pull you into captivity with Me and will make you free – free indeed!

The Scriptures

THE Lord is my light and my salvation; whom shall I fear? the Lord is the strength of my life; of whom shall I be afraid?

One thing have I desired of the Lord, that will I seek after; that I may dwell in the house of the Lord all the days of my life, to behold the beauty of the Lord, and to inquire in his temple.

For in the time of trouble he shall hide me in his pavilion: in the secret of his tabernacle shall he hide me; he shall set me up upon a rock.

Psalm 27:1,4,5

The Lord make his face shine upon thee, and be gracious unto thee:

The Lord lift up his countenance upon thee, and give thee peace.

Numbers 6:25,26

Let us therefore come boldly unto the throne of grace, that we may obtain mercy, and find grace to help in time of need.

Hebrews 4:16

Come unto me, all ye that labour and are heavy laden, and I will give you rest.

Take my yoke upon you, and learn of me; for I am meek and lowly in heart: and ye shall find rest unto your souls.

For my yoke is easy, and my burden is light.

Matthew 11:28-30

And it shall come to pass in that day, that his burden shall be taken away from off thy shoulder, and his yoke from off thy neck, and the yoke shall be destroyed because of the anointing.

Isaiah 10:27

And ye shall know the truth, and the truth shall make you free.

John 8:32

For in him we live, and move, and have our being;

Acts 17:28a

The Prayer

Father, thank You for the place You have prepared for me; that place where my selfish life ends and Your life of love begins in me. I hear Your voice and I come to You. I live in You. I move in You. I have my being in You. Your truth is mine. Your mercy is mine. Your love is mine. Thank You for life and that more abundantly. Before I was, You chose me in Christ Jesus. Now I offer myself a living sacrifice to be yoked together with You, the Lord of my salvation. I praise, honor, and worship You in Spirit and in truth. Amen.

Truth Three

HEAR MY VOICE

The Truth

Listen always to hear My voice. I speak truth. There is a living word that awaits you. Lift up your countenance. Open your heart's eyes and ears and be still. I am your God. I change not. Hear ye Me.

The Scriptures

The eyes of your understanding being enlightened; that ye may know what is the hope of his calling, and what the riches of the glory of his inheritance in the saints,
Ephesians 1:18

Every good gift and every perfect gift is from above, and cometh down from the Father of lights, with whom is no variableness, neither shadow of turning.
James 1:17

But as it is written, Eye hath not seen, nor ear heard, neither have entered into the heart of man, the things which God hath prepared for them that love him.
But God hath revealed them unto us by his Spirit: for the Spirit searcheth all things, yea, the deep things of God.
I Corinthians 2:9,10

God is not a man, that he should lie; neither the son of man, that he should repent: hath he said, and shall he not do it? or hath he spoken, and shall he not make it good?
Numbers 23:19

I am the Lord thy God, which have brought thee out of the land of Egypt, out of the house of bondage.

Thou shall have no other gods before me.

Exodus 20:2,3

Be still, and know that I am God: I will be exalted among the heathen, I will be exalted in the earth.

Psalm 46:10

He that hath an ear, let him hear what the Spirit sayeth unto the churches.

Revelation 3:6

Hear counsel, and receive instruction, that thou mayest be wise in thy latter end.

Proverbs 19:20

It is the spirit that quickeneth; the flesh profiteth nothing: the words that I speak unto you, they are spirit, and they are life.

John 6:63

Blessed is he that readeth, and they that hear the words of this prophecy, and keep those things which are written therein: for the time is at hand.

Revelations 1:3

And ye shall know the truth, and the truth shall make you free.

John 8:32

The Prayer

I come to You, Father, in the name of Jesus. I honor You. I desire to know Your truth and Your will for my life this day. I must be free! Your truth makes me free. I surrender to You as I look upward and inward to where my help comes from. You, O God, are my help. I know that You have a perfect plan for my life. It is a plan for good. I choose to walk in that plan and I choose to trust You and obey You with all my heart. Thank You for Your love. Thank You for a dwelling place in that love. Amen.

Truth Four

LIVE IN UNITY

The Truth

Unity in My body comes as My people seek My face and gravitate toward Me. With Me as your point of focus, your coming to Me brings you, My children, together. The closer you are to Me, the closer you will become to each other. In Me there is a union and all that a *union* represents. Not a local workplace union, but an eternal Kingdom union. A family. My family. So rise above the beggarly elements of the world system and team up with Me for victory in this life. Move from glory to glory. Live in unity as you love me and love one another. This I have commanded of you.

The Scriptures

Can two walk together, unless they be agreed?
Amos 3:3

For where two or three are gathered together in my name, there am I in the midst of them.
Matthew 18:20

They are not of the world, even as I am not of the world.
Sanctify them through thy truth: thy word is truth.
Neither pray I for these alone, but for them also which shall believe on me through their word;
That they all may be one; as thou, Father, art in me, and I in thee, that they also may be one in us: that the world may believe that thou hast sent me.

And the glory which thou gavest me I have given them; that they may be one, even as we are one:

I in them, and thou in me, that they may be made perfect in one; and that the world may know that thou hast sent me, and hast loved them, as thou hast loved me.

John 17:16,17,20-23

I am the vine, ye are the branches: He that abideth in me, and I in him, the same bringeth forth much fruit: for without me ye can do nothing.

John 15:5

But seek ye first the kingdom of God, and his righteousness; and all these things shall be added unto you.

Matthew 6:33

And we know that all things work together for good to them that love God, to them who are the called according to his purpose.

Romans 8:28

ARISE, shine; for thy light is come, and the glory of the Lord is risen upon thee.

Isaiah 60:1

O magnify the Lord with me, and let us exalt his name together.

Psalm 34:3

Now thanks be unto God, which always causes us to triumph in Christ, and maketh manifest the savour of his knowledge by us in every place.

II Corinthians 2:14

Now the God of patience and consolation grant you to be likeminded one toward another according to Christ Jesus:

That ye may with one mind and one mouth glorify God, even the Father of our Lord Jesus Christ.

Wherefore receive one another, as Christ also received us to the glory of God.

Romans 15:5-7

Finally, be ye all of one mind, having compassion one of another, love as brethren, be pitiful, be courteous:

Not rendering evil for evil, or railing for railing: but contrariwise blessing; knowing that ye are thereunto called, that ye should inherit a blessing.

I Peter 3:8,9

The Prayer

Jesus, how I yearn to always live in union with You; even as You are in the Father. I seek You with all of my heart. I praise You with all of my might. I long to hear You call me Your friend. My deep desire is for a closer walk with You - for a more intimate relationship with You. Draw me nearer, Lord Jesus. Thank You for Your love and grace. Thank You for Your precious Holy Spirit. Amen.

Truth Five

GIVE ME CONTROL

The Truth

To use the cruise control on your vehicle relieves you of the concern for manually accelerating as you drive. To cast your cares on Me relieves you of the concern for matters accomplished at Calvary. Cast your cares! Leave your burdens! Let Me have control! CRUISE!

The Scriptures

Why art thou cast down, O my soul? And why are thou disquieted in me? hope thou in God: for I shall yet praise him for the help of his countenance.

Psalm 42:5

Casting all your care upon him; for he careth for you.
I Peter 5:7

Cast thy burden upon the Lord, and he shall sustain thee: he shall never suffer the righteous to be moved.
Psalm 55:22

Come unto me, all ye that labour and are heavy laden, and I will give you rest.
Take my yoke upon you, and learn of me; for I am meek and lowly in heart: and ye shall find rest unto your souls.
For my yoke is easy, and my burden is light.
Matthew 11:28-30

For in him we live, and move, and have our being;
Acts 17:28a

The Lord will perfect that which concerneth me: thy mercy, O Lord, endureth for ever: forsake not the works of thine own hands.
Psalm 138:8

The Prayer

Father, I surrender my all to You. I cast my cares and I abandon the weights that burden me. You receive them, Sir. You take control. I desire to rest in You this day and everyday of my life. I recline and relax in the full comfort of Your love. Thank You for peace that passes all understanding. Thank You that Your joy is my strength. Thank You for the measure of faith. I am the *just*. I live by faith. It is my life of faith that pleases You. So Father, I yield to You. Please take control. Take complete control. In the name of Jesus Christ I pray. Amen.

Truth Six

PRAY FOR LEADERS

The Truth

The king's heart is like a stream of water and I direct it to the place I choose. So remember as you offer up petitions and intercessions for leaders, the hearts of all earthly governmental officials are under My control. You must pray for leaders and those in authority over you that you might live in peace and quiet in the earth.

The Scriptures

Counsel is mine, and sound wisdom: I am understanding; I have strength.

By me kings reign, and princes decree justice.

By me princes rule, and nobles, even all the judges of the earth.

Proverbs 8:14-16

I exhort therefore, that, first of all, supplications, prayers, intercessions, and giving of thanks, be made for all men;

For kings, and for all that are in authority; that we may lead a quiet and peaceable life in all godliness and honesty.

For this is good and acceptable in the sight of God our Saviour;

Who will have all men to be saved, and to come unto the knowledge of the truth.

I Timothy 2:1-4

Submit yourselves to every ordinance of man for the Lord's sake: whether it be to the king, as supreme;

Or unto governors, as unto them that are sent by him for the punishment of evildoers, and for the praise of them that do well.

For so is the will of God, that with well doing ye may put to silence the ignorance of foolish men:

As free, and not using your liberty for a cloke of maliciousness, but as the servants of God.

Honour all men. Love the brotherhood. Fear God. Honour the king.

I Peter 2:13-17

Servants, obey in all things your masters according to the flesh; not with eyeservice, as menpleasers; but in singleness of heart, fearing God:

And whatsoever ye do, do it heartily, as to the Lord, and not unto men;

Knowing that of the Lord ye shall receive the reward of the inheritance: for ye serve the Lord Christ.

Colossians 3:22-24

THE king's heart is in the hand of the Lord, as the rivers of water: he turneth it whithersoever he will.

Proverbs 21:1

The Prayer

Thank you, Father, for the control, direction, and instruction You give to those in positions of authority in the earth. Thank You that they do not suppress or oppress Your sons and daughters. Your word grants us peace that the world cannot give or take away; and perfect peace as our minds are fixed on You. Thank You for loving us and giving Yourself for us that we might have peace in a troubled world; for we are in this world, but not of this world. Our habitation is in Your Kingdom and You, O Lord, You alone are King. Amen.

Truth Seven

SPEAK CREATIVELY

The Truth

You are a spirit being formed in My likeness and My image. I spoke creative words and framed this world. You speak creatively. Your words will frame your world. Guard your hearts. Watch your every word. Be selective about your future. It is in your words!

The Scriptures

Through faith we understand that the worlds were framed by the word of God, so that things which are seen were not made of things which do appear.

Hebrews 11:3

IN the beginning, God created the heaven and the earth.

Genesis 1:1

And God said, Let us make man in our image, after our likeness:

Genesis 1:26a

And the Lord God formed man of the dust of the ground, and breathed into his nostrils the breath of life; and man became a living soul.

Genesis 2:7

And God blessed them, and God said unto them, Be fruitful, and multiply, and replenish the earth, and subdue it: and have dominion over the fish of the sea, and over the foul of the air, and over every living thing that moveth upon the earth.

Genesis 1:28

My son, attend to my words; incline thine ear unto my sayings.

Let them not depart from thine eyes; keep them in the midst of thine heart.

For they are life unto those that find them, and health to all their flesh.

Keep thy heart with all diligence; for out of it are the issues of life.

Put away from thee a froward mouth, and perverse lips put far from thee.

Proverbs 4:20-24

For as he thinketh in his heart, so is he:

Proverbs 23:7a

Hear me now therefore, O ye children, and depart not from the words of my mouth.

Proverbs 5:7

For by thy words thou shalt be justified, and by thy words thou shalt be condemned.

Matthew 12:37

For verily I say unto you, That whosoever shall say unto this mountain, Be thou removed, and be thou cast into the sea; and shall not doubt in his heart, but shall believe that those things which he saith shall come to pass; he shall have whatsoever he saith.

Mark 11:23

Let the words of my mouth, and the meditation of my heart, be acceptable in thy sight, O Lord, my strength, and my redeemer.

Psalm 19:14

The Prayer

Father, how often I hear words from my mouth that I want to retrieve. How slothful I am about the things I say and should not; as well as the things I do not say and should. Help me to think on things that are true, honest, just, pure, lovely, and things that are of good report. As I meditate on Your word and as I pray, please grant me to speak creatively, even as You speak. Let me always say those things which I hear You say. It is Your voice that I will always listen for. It is Your voice that I will hear. It is Your voice that I will always follow. May Your peace that passes all understanding be with me forever. Keep my heart and mind through Christ Jesus, I pray. Amen.

Truth Eight

SEEK MY KINGDOM

The Truth

Seek first My Kingdom above all things. My Kingdom is righteousness, peace and joy in the Holy Ghost. Come into communion with Me and glory in My embrace. My desire is that you prosper and be in good health. My desire is that your soul prospers. Seek my Kingdom first and I grant you the desires of your heart.

The Scriptures

Beloved, I wish above all things that thou mayest prosper and be in health, even as thy soul prospereth.

III John 2

But seek ye first the kingdom of God, and his righteousness; and all these things shall be added unto you.

Matthew 6:33

Fear not, little flock; for it is your Father's good pleasure to give you the kingdom.

Luke 12:32

And when he was demanded of the Pharisees, when the kingdom of God should come, he answered them and said, The kingdom of God cometh not with observation:

Neither shall they say, Lo here! Or, lo there! for, behold, the kingdom of God is within you.

Luke 17:20,21

For the kingdom of God is not meat and drink; but righteousness, and peace, and joy in the Holy Ghost.
Romans 14:17

For the kingdom of God is not in word, but in power.
I Corinthians 4:20

The Prayer

Father God, I want to know You and dwell in Your presence. Thank You that I am reconciled to You by the cross. I will seek You and call upon You. I will find You and honor You. I knock and the door to Your glory opens to me. I pray and You hear and answer my prayers. You show me great and mighty things— exceeding abundantly above all that I ask or think. May the world know You more as they see Your life and love in me. Thank you, Father. Amen.

Truth Nine

YOU ARE MY CHILD

The Truth

You are a child of the King. LIVE LIKE IT!

The Scriptures

Thou art worthy, O Lord, to receive glory and honour and power: for thou hast created all things, and for thy pleasure they are and were created.

Revelation 4:11

And hast made us unto our God kings and priests: and we shall reign on the earth.

Revelation 5:10

Blessed be the God and Father of our Lord Jesus Christ, who hath blessed us with all spiritual blessings in heavenly places in Christ:

According as he hath chosen us in him before the foundation of the world, that we should be holy and without blame before him in love:

Having predestinated us unto the adoption of children by Jesus Christ to himself, according to the good pleasure of his will,

To the praise of the glory of his grace, wherein he hath made us accepted in the beloved.

In whom also we have obtained an inheritance, being predestinated according to the purpose of him who worketh all things after the counsel of his own will:

That we should be to the praise of his glory, who first trusted in Christ.

Ephesians 1:3-6;11,12

Be ye therefore perfect, as your father which is in heaven is perfect.

Matthew 5:48

Then shall the King say unto them on his right hand, Come, ye blessed of my Father, inherit the kingdom prepared for you from the foundation of the world.

Matthew 25:34

The Prayer

Christ Jesus, You are my King. You have received me into Your family and into Your Kingdom. I am eternally honored. I am eternally grateful. Thank You. Amen.

Truth Ten

PRAY

The Truth

I have called you to pray for each other. Prayer is vitally important to your lives. So pray without ceasing. Remember, I am interceding for you. You must intercede for each other. PRAY!

The Scriptures

But ye, beloved, building up yourselves on your most holy faith, praying in the Holy Ghost,

Keep yourselves in the love of God, looking for the mercy of our Lord Jesus Christ unto eternal life.

Jude 20,21

Pray without ceasing.

I Thessalonians 5:17

Hereby perceive we the love of God, because he laid down his life for us: and we ought to lay down our lives for the brethren.

I John 3:16

And he spake a parable unto them to this end, that men ought always to pray, and not to faint;

Luke 18:1

Call unto me, and I will answer thee, and shew thee great and mighty things,

Jeremiah 33:3a

Be careful for nothing; but in every thing by prayer and supplication with thanksgiving let your requests be made known unto God.

Philippians 4:6

And whatsoever we ask, we receive of him, because we keep his commandments, and do those things that are pleasing in his sight.

I John 3:22

And the Lord said, Simon, Simon, behold, Satan hath desired to have you, that he may sift you as wheat:

But I have prayed for thee, that thy faith fail not: and when thou art converted, strengthen thy brethren.

Luke 22:31,32

Likewise the Spirit also helpeth our infirmities: for we know not what we should pray for as we ought: but the Spirit itself maketh intercession for us with groanings which cannot be uttered.

And he that searcheth the hearts knoweth what is the mind of the Spirit, because he maketh intercession for the saints according to the will of God.

Romans 8:26,27

The Prayer

Thank You, Lord Jesus, that I can and I will pray for others. My life in You shall always be one of considering others above myself and loving them as I love myself. Thank You that You are praying for me. Your very presence positionally at the right hand of the Father is in representation of me. You are my wonderful Lord and Savior, and my life is hid in You. Amen.

Truth Eleven

OFFER PRAISE AND WORSHIP

The Truth

Do not bow down to any graven image or ungodly thing. Do not fear the fiery furnace. Do not fear the lion's den. Put your trust in Me. Offer up prayers and supplications with thanksgiving. Offer up praise and worship. I dwell in your praises. My glory prevails in your worship.

The Scriptures

I am the Lord: that is my name: and my glory will I not give to another, neither my praise to graven images.

Isaiah 42:8

YE shall make you no idols nor graven image, neither rear you up a standing image, neither shall ye set up any image of stone in your land, to bow down unto it: for I am the Lord your God.

Leviticus 26:1

But thou art holy, O thou that inhabitest the praises of Israel.

Psalm 22:3

Enter into his gates with thanksgiving, and into his courts with praise: be thankful unto him, and bless his name.

Psalm 100:4

Praying always with all prayer and supplication in the Spirit, and watching thereunto with all perseverance and supplication for all saints;

Ephesians 6:18

BEHOLD, bless ye the Lord, all ye servants of the Lord, which by night stand in the house of the Lord.
Lift up you hands in the sanctuary, and bless the Lord.
The Lord that made heaven and earth bless thee out of Zion.

Psalm 134

PRAISE ye the Lord. Praise ye the name of the Lord; praise him, O ye servants of the Lord.

Psalm 135:1

MAKE a joyful noise unto God, all ye lands:
Sing forth the honour of his name: make his praise glorious.

Psalm 66:1,2

PRAISE ye the Lord. Praise God in his sanctuary: praise him in the firmament of his power.
Praise him for his mighty acts: praise him according to his excellent greatness.
Let every thing that hath breath praise the Lord. Praise ye the Lord.

Psalm 150:1,2,6

The Prayer

With all of my being, Father, I trust You, honor You, praise You, and worship You. I do not fear the fiery furnace or the lion's den. I have faith in You to deliver. You have shown me Your goodness, grace and mercy. Thank You for dwelling in my praises. You are great and You are awesome. Thank You for the overflow of every well of salvation. I will always be mindful that in You I have victory over every circumstance and in every situation in my life. Thank You for victory. Amen.

Truth Twelve

LOVE AS I LOVE

The Truth

Even the least of them are My children. Do good to them. Whatever you do to them, count it done also to Me. Reach out with your love and touch them as I reach out with My love and touch you. You are made in My likeness and image, to love as I love.

The Scriptures

Then Peter opened his mouth, and said, Of a truth I perceive that God is no respecter of persons:

Acts 10:34

My brethren, have not the faith of our Lord Jesus Christ, the Lord of glory, with respect of persons.

For if there come unto your assembly a man with a gold ring, in goodly apparel, and there come in also a poor man in vile raiment;

And ye have respect to him that weareth the gay clothing, and say unto him, Sit thou here in a good place; and say to the poor, Stand thou there, or sit here under my footstool:

Are ye not then partial in yourselves, and are become judges of evil thoughts?

Hearken, my beloved brethren, Hath not God chosen the poor of this world rich in faith, and heirs of the kingdom which he hath promised to them that love him?

James 2:1-5

Then were there brought unto him little children, that he should put his hands on them, and pray: and the disciples rebuked them.

But Jesus said, Suffer little children, and forbid them not, to come unto me: for of such is the kingdom of heaven.
Matthew 19:13,14

But whoso shall offend one of these little ones which believe in me, it were better for him that a millstone were hanged about his neck, and that he were drowned in the depth of the sea.
Matthew 18:6

A new commandment I give unto you, That ye love one another; as I have loved you, that ye also love one another.
John 13:34

Keep yourselves in the love of God, looking for the mercy of our Lord Jesus Christ unto eternal life.
Jude v. 21

The Prayer

Thank You, Father, that even when I am not prepared to love others and I find myself judging them and setting worldly standards, You teach me to love. With a heart willing to obey You, with a mind renewed to Your word, and with my eyes focused on You, I extend to others not only my heart, but also my hand. Thank You that Christ reigns in me and leads me in a life of love - Your love. Amen.

Truth Thirteen

CELEBRATE LIFE

The Truth

This is a day that I have given to you. Rejoice and be exceedingly glad in it. Celebrate life today! I came that you might have life—a good life—an abundant life. I want you to prosper and be in health, even as your soul prospers. Now is the day of salvation. So celebrate life today!

The Scriptures

The thief cometh not, but for to steal, and to kill, and to destroy: I am come that they might have life, and that they might have it more abundantly.

John 10:10

Rejoice evermore.
Pray without ceasing.
In everything give thanks: for this is the will of God in Christ Jesus concerning you.

I Thessalonians 5:16-18

For whoso findeth me findeth life, and shall obtain favor of the Lord.

Proverbs 8:35

The blessing of the Lord, it maketh rich, and he addeth no sorry with it.

Proverbs 10:22

We then, as workers together with him, beseech you also that ye receive not the grace of God in vain.

(For he saith, I have heard thee in a time accepted, and in the day of salvation have I succoured thee: behold, now is the accepted time; behold, now is the day of salvation.)

II Corinthians 6:1,2

Holding forth the word of life; that I may rejoice in the day of Christ, that I have not run in vain, neither laboured in vain.

Philippians 2:16

The Prayer

Thank You, Father, for giving Jesus to redeem me. His finished work on the cross was death that I might have eternal life. It was sickness for my healing and sorrow for my peace. He took my sin that I might become Your righteousness in Him. I praise You. You have prepared a place in You for me that where You are, I may be also. Keep me in Your care as I celebrate the good life – the God life – today and everyday. Amen.

Truth Fourteen

REPENT AND OBEY

The Truth

Repent and obey. I will deliver you without delay. So arise and go forth as you hear the word plainly from Me. A treasure of empowerment to prosper is yours and your prayers are answered because of your obedience.

The Scriptures

In those days came John the Baptist, preaching in the wilderness of Judaea,

And saying, Repent ye: for the kingdom of heaven is at hand.

Matthew 3:1,2

If we confess our sins, he is faithful and just to forgive us our sins, and to cleanse us from all unrighteousness.

I John 1:9

I will hear what God the Lord will speak: for he will speak peace unto his people, and to his saints: but let them not turn again to folly.

Psalm 85:8

Blessed be the God and Father of our Lord Jesus Christ, who hath blessed us with all spiritual blessings in heavenly places in Christ:

Ephesians 1:3

And whatsoever we ask, we receive of him, because we keep his commandments, and do those things that are pleasing in his sight.

I John 3:22

And this is the confidence that we have in him, that, if we ask any thing according to his will, he heareth us:
And if we know that he hear us, whatsoever we ask, we know that we have the petitions that we desired of him.

I John 5;14,15

If ye be willing and obedient, ye shall eat the good of the land:

Isaiah 1:19

The Prayer

Thank You, Father, for Your Holy Spirit. How wonderful You are. You hear and You answer prayer. You are faithful to forgive my sins when I confess them to You. You make the crooked paths straight before me. You raise up the valleys and bring down the hills. You provide streams of water in the dry places. You have already blessed me with every spiritual blessing in heavenly places. These blessings are manifested in my life. Thank You for living Your life through me. Thank You that it is in You that I live and move and have my being. Daily I listen for Your voice. Daily I will obey. Surely goodness and mercy shall follow me all of my days. In the name of Jesus the Christ. Amen.

Truth Fifteen

STAY ON COURSE

The Truth

Follow Me as I lead you. Stay on course. Stay with Me and in Me. Remember that I will never fail or forsake you. Now, you do likewise; do not fail or forsake Me. Together we can and will move the mountains that stand before you. Satan will come, but he finds nothing in you. You are in Me; hidden under My wings and sheltered in the cleft of the Rock. My angels watch over you. Stay on course.

The Scriptures

THE Lord is my shepherd; I shall not want.

He maketh me to lie down in green pastures: he leadeth me beside the still waters.

He restoreth my soul: he leadeth me in the paths of righteousness for his name's sake.

Psalm 23:1-3

The steps of a good man are ordered by the Lord: and he delighteth in his way.

Though he fall, he shall not be utterly cast down: for the Lord upholdeth him with his hand.

I have been young, and now am old; yet have I not seen the righteous forsaken, nor his seed begging bread.

He is ever merciful, and lendeth; and his seed is blessed.

Psalm 37:23-26

Wherefore I beseech you, be ye followers of me.

I Corinthians 4:16

BE ye therefore followers of God, as dear children;
Ephesians 5:1

There shall not any man be able to stand before thee all the days of thy life: as I was with Moses, so I will be with thee: I will not fail thee, nor forsake thee.
Joshua 1:5

If ye abide in me, and my words abide in you, ye shall ask what ye will, and it shall be done unto you.
John 15:7

For verily I say unto you, That whosoever shall say unto this mountain, Be thou removed, and be thou cast into the sea; and shall not doubt in his heart, but shall believe that those things which he saith shall come to pass; he shall have whatsoever he saith.
Mark 11:23

I will say of the Lord, He is my refuge and my fortress: my God; in him will I trust.
Surely he shall deliver thee from the snare of the fowler, and from the noisome pestilence.
He shall cover thee with his feathers, and under his wings shalt thou trust: his truth shall be thy shield and buckler.
For he shall give his angels charge over thee, to keep thee in all thy ways.
Psalm 91:2-4, 11

The Prayer

Father, I thank You that You are with me always. You never leave me, fail me, or forsake me. I give no place to the enemy—except under my feet. I speak Your word over my life situations and circumstances and every one of them is subject to the matchless name of Jesus. They must bow! Lead me and I shall follow. Send me and I shall go. Amen.

Truth Sixteen

YIELD TO MY SPIRIT

The Truth

Yield to My Spirit. My Spirit abides with you to keep you from the onslaught of the enemy. The enemy seeks to attack your will and emotions and rush upon you to weaken you. Be of good courage. My Spirit is within you to deliver you and lead you into all truth. My Spirit will restore calm to your life. Yield! Trust!

The Scriptures

Be strong and of a good courage:
Only be thou strong and very courageous, that thy mayest observe to do according to all the law, which Moses my servant commanded thee: turn not from it to the right hand or to the left, that thou mayest prosper withersoever thou goest.

Joshua 1:6a,7

Because thou hast made the Lord, which is my refuge, even the most High, thy habitation;
There shall no evil befall the, neither shall any plague come nigh thy dwelling.

Psalm 91:9,10

When a man's ways please the Lord, he maketh even his enemies to be at peace with him.

Proverbs 16:7

For he is our peace, who hath made both one, and hath broken down the middle wall of partition between us;
Ephesians 2:14

Be sober, be vigilant; because your adversary the devil, as a roaring lion, walketh about, seeking whom he may devour:
I Peter 5:8

For which cause we faint not; but though our outward man perish, yet the inward man is renewed day by day.
II Corinthians 4:16

Howbeit when he, the Spirit of truth, is come, he will guide you into all truth: for he shall not speak of himself; but whatsoever he shall hear, that shall he speak: and he will shew you things to come.
John 16:13

Know ye not, that to whom ye yield yourselves servants to obey, his servants ye are to whom ye obey; whether of sin unto death, or of obedience unto righteousness?
Romans 6:16

Have I not commanded thee? Be strong and of a good courage; be not afraid, neither be thou dismayed: for the Lord thy God is with thee whithersoever thou goest.
Joshua 1:9

Trust in the Lord with all thine heart; and lean not unto thine own understanding.

In all thy ways acknowledge him, and he shall direct thy paths.

Proverbs 3:5,6

The Prayer

I surrender to You, Father. I offer all that I am and all that I have into Your hands. I receive the blessedness of Your Spirit in my life to bring strength in my weakness. In You, my fears are eradicated and replaced with faith, confidence, and trust. I am led and guided into all truth. Thank You for Your Spirit working <u>in</u> me, <u>with</u> me, <u>for</u> me, <u>through</u> me and <u>over</u> me. Amen.

Truth Seventeen

ABIDE IN ME

The Truth

I am the vine. You are the branches. Abide in me. I am the beginning. I am the end. I Am…I Am…

The Scriptures

Abide in me, and I in you. As the branch cannot bear fruit of itself, except it abide in the vine; no more can ye, except ye abide in me.

I am the vine, ye are the branches: He that abideth in me, and I in him, the same bringeth forth much fruit: for without me ye can do nothing.

If ye abide in me, and my words abide in you, ye shall ask what ye will, and it shall be done unto you.

John 15:4,5,7

He that saith he abideth in him ought himself also so to walk, even as he walked.

I John 2:6

If ye keep my commandments, ye shall abide in my love; even as I have kept my Father's commandments, and abide in his love.

John 15:10

And he that keepeth his commandments dwelleth in him, and he in him. And hereby we know that he abideth in us, by the Spirit which he hath given us.

I John 3:24

I am a companion of all them that fear thee, and of them that keep thy precepts.

Psalm 119:63

For ye are dead, and your life is hid with Christ in God.
Colossians 3:3

And he said unto me, It is done. I am Alpha and Omega, the beginning and the end. I will give unto him that is athirst of the fountain of the water of life freely.

Revelation 21:6

And God said unto Moses, I AM THAT I AM: and he said, Thus shalt thou say unto the children of Israel, I AM hath sent me unto you.

Exodus 3:14

The Prayer

Thank You, Father, that You are the great I AM. You are the I AM of Moses' burning bush. You are the I AM of Aaron's rod that buddeth. You are the I AM in Miriam's tambourine. You are the I AM on the Red Sea roadway. You are the I AM for the lame man at the Gate Beautiful. You are the I AM with Paul before Agrippa. You are the I AM in John on the Isle of Patmos. You are the I AM in my life. You are the I AM of eternity. I give my life as a praise to You in the earth. I am an ambassador of the great I AM. Thank You, Father. Amen.

Truth Eighteen

DIE TO SELF

The Truth

Die daily to self. Mortify the flesh. Bring your life into subjection to My word. Stay inside of Me. Find your peace and protection in Me. The prince of the power of the air will seek you. He goes about as a roaring lion to steal, kill and destroy. Hold on to My word. As you die to self, My word is life and nourishment for the new you -- the resurrected life of your spirit.

The Scriptures

He that loveth his life shall lose it; and he that hateth his life in this world shall keep it unto life eternal.

John 12:25

For whosoever will save his life shall lose it; but whosoever shall lose his life for my sake and the gospel's, the same shall save it.

For what shall it profit a man, if he shall gain the whole world, and lose his own soul?

Or what shall a man give in exchange for his soul?

Mark 8:35-37

Knowing this, that our old man is crucified with him, that the body of sin might be destroyed, that henceforth we should not serve sin.

For he that is dead is freed from sin.

Now if we be dead with Christ, we believe that we shall also live with him:

Knowing that Christ being raised from the dead dieth no more; death hath no more dominion over him.

Romans 6:6-9

I am crucified with Christ: nevertheless I live; yet not I, but Christ liveth in me: and the life which I now live in the flesh I live by the faith of the Son of God, who loved me, and gave himself for me.

Galatians 2:20

Set your affection on things above, not on things on the earth.

For ye are dead, and your life is hid with Christ in God.

When Christ, who is our life, shall appear, then shall ye also appear with him in glory.

Mortify therefore your members which are upon the earth;

Colossians 3:2-5a

For if ye live after the flesh, ye shall die: but if ye through the Spirit do mortify the deeds of the body, ye shall live.

Romans 8:13

Be sober, be vigilant; because your adversary the devil, as a roaring lion, walketh about, seeking whom he may devour:

I Peter 5:8

Submit yourselves therefore to God. Resist the devil, and he will flee from you.

James 4:7

And let the peace of God rule in your hearts, to the which also ye are called in one body; and be ye thankful.

Colossians 3:15

For the arms of the wicked shall be broken: but the Lord upholdeth the righteous.

The Lord knoweth the days of the upright: and their inheritance shall be for ever.

They shall not be ashamed in the evil time: and in the days of famine they shall be satisfied.

Psalm 37:17-19

Depart from evil, and do good; and dwell for evermore.

For the Lord loveth judgment, and forsaketh not his saints; they are preserved for ever: but the seed of the wicked shall be cut off.

The righteous shall inherit the land, and dwell therein for ever.

Psalm 37:27-29

The Prayer

Lord, I mortify the deeds of this flesh. I open up Your word which is life to me. I consume it and am refreshed. Then, I stand against the tactics and antics of the enemy with a renewed mind. I am fully clothed in the armour of God. When I have stood, I will continue to stand; not alone, but in You. Thank You that in a blaze of glory, You raise up a standard against my enemy and You manifest the victory for me. Thank You, Father. Amen.

Truth Nineteen

TRUST ME

The Truth

Speak My words and I perform them. You expound on the "what" of your prayers. I will determine the "how" for the manifestation. Do not be afraid. Trust Me.

The Scriptures

And this is the confidence that we have in him, that, if we ask any thing according to his will, he heareth us:

And if we know that he hear us, whatsoever we ask, we know that we have the petitions that we desired of him.

I John 5:14,15

Then the Lord put forth his hand, and touched my mouth. And the Lord said unto me, Behold, I have put my words in thy mouth.

Then said the Lord unto me, Thou hast well seen: for I will hasten my word to perform it.

Jeremiah 1:9,12

Be not afraid of sudden fear, neither of the desolation of the wicked, when it cometh.

For the Lord shall be thy confidence, and shall keep thy foot from being taken.

Proverbs 3:25,26

Trust in the Lord with all thine heart; and lean not unto thine own understanding.

Proverbs 3:5

For God hath not given us a spirit of fear; but of power, and of love, and of a sound mind.

II Timothy 1:7

So shall thy barns be filled with plenty, and thy presses shall burst out with new wine.

Proverbs 3:10

The Prayer

Thank You, Father, for every opportunity to come and reason together with You. You said that if I come to You, You would not cast me out. My life and confidence are in You and You alone. You are my God. I make known to You my petitions, supplications and intercessions, then I am still - to see Your glory revealed. Amen.

Truth Twenty

YOU ARE AN OVERCOMER

The Truth

The system of My word brings life. The system of the world brings death. Satan is the author of death. Your fight is in the arena of faith. There the victory is yours. You are an overcomer. You overcome by the blood of the Lamb and the word of your testimony. So let My words be your words. Overcome!

The Scriptures

Let the words of my mouth, and the meditation of my heart, be acceptable in thy sight, O Lord, my strength, and my redeemer.

Psalm 19:14

So shall my word be that goeth forth out of my mouth: it shall not return unto me void, but it shall accomplish that which I please, and it shall prosper in the thing whereto I sent it.

Isaiah 55:11

...and out of his mouth went a sharp two-edged sword: and his countenance was as the sun shineth in his strength.

Revelation 1:16b

For the word of God is quick, and powerful, and sharper than any two-edged sword, piercing even to the dividing asunder of soul and spirit, and of the joints and marrow, and is a discerner of the thoughts and intents of the heart.

Hebrews 4:12

Be not overcome of evil, but overcome evil with good.
Romans 12:21

Ye are of God, little children, and have overcome them: because greater is he that is in you, than he that is in the world.
I John 4:4

My son, attend to my words; incline thine ear unto my sayings.

Let them not depart from thine eyes; keep them in the midst of thine heart.

For they are life unto those that find them, and health to all their flesh.
Proverbs 4:20-22

Fight the good fight of faith, lay hold on eternal life, whereunto thou art also called, and hast professed a good profession before many witnesses.
I Timothy 6:12

The Prayer

Father, let Your words in my mouth be acceptable to You. May they flow up as a sweet smelling fragrance before Your throne. May they comfort, edify and exhort the saints. May they be as building blocks in Your Kingdom. May they bring victory in every area of my life as I fight the good fight of faith – standing steadfastly on Your word and overcoming by the blood of Jesus. Amen.

Truth Twenty-one

MY POWER CHANNEL

The Truth

You are a conduit through which my power flows from heavenly places to earth. Think not a small conduit of one-inch diameter, but think huge dam-sized concrete channels. You think big and I think even bigger! Let My life, power and blessings flow into you and through you at all times. You are My child. You are my power channel.

The Scriptures

But ye shall receive power, after that the Holy Ghost is come upon you: and ye shall be witnesses unto me both in Jerusalem, and in all Judaea, and in Samaria, and unto the uttermost part of the earth.

Acts 1:8

Also I heard the voice of the Lord, saying, Whom shall I send, and who will go for us? Then said I, Here am I; send me.

Isaiah 6:8

And he said unto them, Go ye into all the world, and preach the gospel to every creature.

He that believeth and is baptized shall be saved; but he that believeth not shall be damned.

And these signs shall follow them that believe; In my name shall they cast out devils; they shall speak with new tongues;

They shall take up serpents; and if they drink any deadly thing, it shall not hurt them; they shall lay hands on the sick, and they shall recover.

Mark 16:15-18

Now unto him that is able to do exceeding abundantly above all that we ask or think, according to the power that worketh in us,

Unto him be glory in the church by Christ Jesus throughout all ages, world without end. Amen

Ephesians 3:20,21

The Prayer

Thank You, Father, that I am Your vessel in the earth. I submit myself to be used according to Your plan which was established for my life from the foundation of the world. I desire to occupy the space You have provided for me in the earth and to fulfill my purpose for Your Kingdom. In the name of Jesus.Amen.

Truth Twenty-two

VICTORY

The Truth

As a believer in Christ, the power that you have is in My word. The authority is in the name of Jesus. The sanctification is in the covering of the blood and the work is by the Holy Spirit and the angels. The Word, the Name, the Blood. The Power, the Authority, the Covering. Victory!

The Scriptures

If ye abide in me, and my words abide in you, ye shall ask what ye will, and it shall be done unto you.

John 15:7

Nevertheless I tell you the truth; It is expedient for you that I go away: for if I go not away, the Comforter will not come unto you; but if I depart, I will send him unto you.

John 16:7

But ye shall receive power, after that the Holy Ghost is come upon you:

Acts 1:8a

Howbeit when he, the Spirit of truth, is come, he will guide you into all truth: for he shall not speak of himself; but whatsoever he shall hear, that shall he speak: and he will shew you things to come.

He shall glorify me: for he shall receive of mine, and shall shew it unto you.

John 16:13,14

But now in Christ Jesus ye who sometimes were far off are made nigh by the blood of Christ.

Ephesians 2:13

And whatsoever ye shall ask in my name, that will I do, that the Father may be glorified in the Son.
If ye shall ask anything in my name, I will do it.

John 14:13,14

And now, Lord, behold their threatenings: and grant unto thy servants, that with all boldness they may speak thy word,
By stretching forth thy hand to heal; and that signs and wonders may be done by the name of thy holy child Jesus.

Acts 4:29,30

Are they not all ministering spirits, sent forth to minister for them who shall be heirs of salvation?

Hebrews 1:14

The Prayer

Father, I thank You for Your word. All things consist by it. All creation exists by it. I desire always to be yoked together with Jesus; whose name is above all names, whose blood cleanses me from all unrighteousness, and whose Spirit leads me into all truth. I love You, Lord. Amen.

Truth Twenty-three

YOU CHOOSE

The Truth

You choose. Just as you, in times past, opened a door of doubt and unbelief and allowed the enemy to come into your life and reek havoc; so shall you, in this day, open the door of faith and trust to allow Christ into your life to bring a flow of blessing. A sinful life honors satan. A holy life honors Christ. You choose!

The Scriptures

AND it shall come to pass, if thou shall hearken diligently unto the voice of the Lord thy God, to observe and to do all his commandments which I command thee this day, that the Lord thy God will set thee on high above all nations of the earth:

And all these blessings shall come on thee, and overtake thee, if thou shall hearken unto the voice of the Lord thy God.

Deuteronomy 28:1,2

Bring ye all the tithes into the storehouse, that there may be meat in mine house, and prove me now herewith, saith the Lord of hosts, if I will not open you the windows of heaven, and pour you out a blessing, that there shall not be room enough to receive it.

Malachi 3:10

Submit yourselves therefore to God. Resist the devil, and he will flee from you.

James 4:7

For ye are bought with a price: therefore glorify God in your body, and in your spirit, which are God's.

I Corinthians 6:20

And if it seem evil unto you to serve the Lord, choose you this day whom ye will serve; whether the gods which your fathers served that were on the other side of the flood, or the gods of the Amorites, in whose land ye dwell: but as for me and my house, we will serve the Lord.

Joshua 24:15

The Prayer

Thank You, Father, that satan is already defeated and has been publicly displayed as a spectacle in the presence of his own. As I draw near to You, I resist him in the name of Jesus. He flees from me in terror. I submit myself to You; I hear Your words and I obey them. The blessing of Abraham is mine as You empower me to prosper – spirit, soul, and body. Amen.

Truth Twenty-four

MY GIFTS - SALVATION AND FAITH

The Truth

If you purchased a ticket and received a boarding pass on an aircraft, you would wait confidently in line at the gate. Your seat is reserved. You are assured of passage. Now know this. Your ticket with Me is salvation through Jesus Christ. Your boarding pass is faith in His finished work at Calvary. You are clothed in My righteousness and seated with Christ in heavenly places. The price is paid in full. The cost was the blood of Jesus. These are My gifts to you. Salvation! Faith!

The Scriptures

For God so loved the world, that he gave his only begotten Son, that whosoever believeth in him should not perish, but have everlasting life.

John 3:16

What? Know ye not that your body is the temple of the Holy Ghost which is in you, which ye have of God, and ye are not your own?
For ye are bought with a price: therefore glorify God in your body, and in your spirit, which are God's.

I Corinthians 6:19,20

For ye have need of patience, that, after ye have done the will of God, ye might receive the promise.

Hebrews 10:36

...for he that cometh to God must believe that he is, and that he is a rewarder of them that diligently seek him.

Hebrews 11:6b

NOW faith is the substance of things hoped for, the evidence of things not seen.

Hebrews 11:1

So then faith cometh by hearing, and hearing by the word of God.

Romans 10:17

The Prayer

Thank You, Father, for giving Your only Son to redeem me from sin and the curse of the law. I will always be confident in my salvation and will share Your love with those I encounter in my life. I will proclaim the good news and speak peace to Your creation. In Jesus name. Amen.

Truth Twenty-five

I AM YOUR VICTORY

The Truth

I have been to your end. Now I am come to your beginning to take you to your end. I will walk with you on your forward journey. If you turn aside, I cannot. I will wait for you to return to Me; then we will go on together. When trials, tribulations, and problems come, I am your insulation. Sin cannot touch me. Stay in me. You will experience salvation in every area of your life. In Me, you have victory over the world. I am your victory.

The Scriptures

He hath shewed thee, O man, what is good; and what doth the Lord require of thee, but to do justly, and to love mercy, and to walk humbly with thy God?

Micah 6:8

Therefore also now, saith the Lord, turn ye even to me with all your heart, and with fasting, and with weeping, and with mourning.

Joel 2:12

Then shall ye call upon me, and ye shall go and pray unto me, and I will hearken unto you.
And ye shall seek me, and find me, when ye shall search for me with all your heart.

Jeremiah 29:12,13

Go ye therefore, and teach all nations, baptizing them in the name of the Father, and of the Son, and of the Holy Ghost:

Teaching them to observe all things whatsoever I have commanded you: and, lo, I am with you alway, even unto the end of the world.

Matthew 28:19,20

These things I have spoken unto you, that in me ye might have peace. In the world ye shall have tribulation: but be of good cheer; I have overcome the world.

John 16:33

But thanks be to God, which giveth us the victory through our Lord Jesus Christ.

I Corinthians 15:57

The Prayer

Thank You, Father, that You give me Your Holy Spirit to lead and guide me in every area of my life. I will not turn away to the right or to the left, but will keep my heart fixed on You. Thank You that the rain of Your Spirit keeps falling on me and the wells of my salvation go beyond full to overflowing. There is a river of life in me. There is more than enough. I take the overflow to share on my forward journey in the Kingdom. Thank You that I am complete and victorious in You and made perfect in Jesus Christ. Amen.

Truth Twenty-six

The Truth

My words spoken with your mouth are seeds of faith. Plant them! Do not uproot your good seed with doubt, fear and unbelief. Planted, watered, and nurtured, your seeds will produce roots to grow deep and send up sustenance from the foundation to the super-structure. You are guaranteed a Kingdom harvest from My word. Reap in joy.

The Scriptures

While the earth remaineth, seedtime and harvest, and cold and heat, and summer and winter, and day and night shall not cease.

Genesis 8:22

Be not deceived; God is not mocked: for whatsoever a man soweth, that shall he also reap.

And let us not be weary in well doing: for in due season we shall reap if we faint not.

Galatians 6:7,9

For God hath not given us the spirit of fear; but of power, and of love, and of a sound mind.

Hold fast the form of sound words, which thou hast heard of me, in faith and love which is in Christ Jesus.

That good thing which was committed unto thee keep by the Holy Ghost which dwelleth in us.

II Timothy 1:7, 13,14

And he said, So is the kingdom of God, as if a man should cast seed into the ground;

And should sleep, and rise night and day, and the seed should spring and grow up, he knoweth not how.

For the earth bringeth forth fruit of herself; first the blade, then the ear, after that the full corn in the ear.

But when the fruit is brought forth, immediately he putteth in the sickle, because the harvest is come.

Mark 4:26-29

The Lord shall increase you more and more, you and your children.

Psalm 115:14

The Prayer

Thank You, Father, that the words I speak are spirit and life. My words, which are Your words, produce after their own kind. You stand behind them and You perform them. They are creative. They are seeds going forth to produce. Thank You for the harvest. In the name of Jesus. Amen.

Truth Twenty-seven

COME AND RECEIVE

The Truth

Do not try to coax Me to send blessings to you. Have I not given you Jesus? Did He not die for you? Come unto Me. Come into My Kingdom. Come and receive what you need and what you desire. Seek My Kingdom first. That is how you get the *things*. They will be added unto you. Come.

The Scriptures

Every good gift and every perfect gift is from above, and cometh down from the Father of lights, with whom is no variableness, neither shadow of turning.

James 1:17

Blessed be the God and Father of our Lord Jesus Christ, who hath blessed us with all spiritual blessings in heavenly places in Christ:

Ephesians 1:3

In whom are hid all the treasures of wisdom and knowledge.

Colossians 2:3

Who hath delivered us from the power of darkness, and hath translated us into the kingdom of his dear Son:

Colossians 1:13

But seek ye first the kingdom of God, and his righteousness; and all these things shall be added unto you.

Matthew 6:33

And ye shall seek me, and find me, when ye shall search for me with all your heart.

Jeremiah 29:13

Giving thanks unto the Father, which hath made us meet to be partakers of the inheritance of the saints in light:

Colossians 1:12

The blessing of the Lord, it maketh rich, and he addeth no sorry with it.

Proverbs 10:22

The Prayer

Thank You, Father, for every good and every perfect gift. Thank You that there is no variableness or shadow of turning with You. Thank You that You reveal to me Your wisdom and knowledge. I will seek Your Kingdom and seek Your face with my whole heart. I love You and I thank You that You allow me to live in Your love. That is where I desire to be always. Amen.

Truth Twenty-eight

MY WORD WILL ENDURE

The Truth

You must not allow yourself to drown in the trivia and mediocrity of an earthly existence. You were created for Kingdom living. Grab a plank. Consider that the plank is My Son and My Son is My Word and My Word is My promise to you. Hold on to it. You cannot drown. My Word will not sink. My Word will not fail. My Word will endure forever.

The Scriptures

IN the beginning was the Word, and the Word was with God, and the Word was God.

John 1:1

My son, if sinners entice thee, consent thou not.

Proverbs 1:10

Love not the world, neither the things that are in the world. If any man love the world, the love of the father is not in him.

For all that is in the world, the lust of the flesh, the lust of the eyes, and the pride of life, is not of the Father, but is of the world.

And the world passeth away, and the lust thereof: but he that doeth the will of God abideth for ever.

I John 2:15-17

Wherefore lay apart all filthiness and superfluity of naughtiness, and receive with meekness the engrafted word, which is able to save your souls.

But be ye doers of the word, and not hearers only, deceiving your own selves.

James 1:21,22

There hath no temptation taken you but such as is common to man: but God is faithful, who will not suffer you to be tempted above that ye are able; but will with the temptation also make a way to escape, that ye may be able to bear it.

I Corinthians 10:13

For verily I say unto you, Till heaven and earth pass, one jot or one tittle shall in no wise pass from the law, till all be fulfilled.

Matthew 5:18

Thy word is a lamp unto my feet, and a light unto my path.

Psalms 119:105

The Prayer

Thank You, Father, for Your word which sustains me in the dark hours of storm and shipwreck. Thank You that there is no temptation that comes to me but such as is common in the life of man. Thank You that You are with me always; for in You I live and move and have my being. I can hold on to You for life – I will hold on to You for life – the abundant life in Christ Jesus. Amen.

Truth Twenty-nine

STAND

The Truth

The battle of your life is Mine; the victory of life is yours. I have already won the battle. I have given the victory to you. So adorn yourself with the full armour of God. Remember that your only action is to fight the good fight of faith and to stand in victory. Stand – stand – stand!

The Scriptures

And he said, Hearken ye, all Judah, and ye inhabitants of Jerusalem, and thou King Jehoshaphat, thus saith the Lord unto you, Be not afraid nor dismayed by reason of this great multitude; for the battle is not yours, but God's.

II Chronicles 20:15

And Moses said unto the people, Fear ye not, stand still, and see the salvation of the Lord, which he will shew to you to day: for the Egyptians whom ye have seen to day, ye shall see them again no more for ever.

The Lord shall fight for you, and ye shall hold your peace.

Exodus 14:13,14

Put on the whole armour of God, that ye may be able to stand against the wiles of the devil.

For we wrestle not against flesh and blood, but against principalities, against powers, against the rulers of the darkness of this world, against spiritual wickedness in high places.

Wherefore take unto you the whole armour of God, that ye may be able to withstand in the evil day, and having done all, to stand.

Ephesians 6:11-13

Fight the good fight of faith, lay hold on eternal life, whereunto thou art also called, and hast professed a good profession before many witnesses.

I Timothy 6:12

Fear thou not; for I am with thee: be not dismayed; for I am thy God: I will strengthen thee; yea, I will help thee; yea, I will uphold thee with the right hand of my righteousness.

Isaiah 41:10

The Prayer

Father, I thank You. You have provided victory for me and given me full salvation. My faith and trust are in You. I am strong in You and I adorn myself with the full armour of Your word. I stand today and will remain standing; praying always with all prayer for all the saints, and waiting for the day when Jesus returns for His church. In the name of Christ. Amen.

Truth Thirty

EXPECT THE BEST

The Truth

I am come that you might have life and that life more abundantly. I AM is the Lord your God. As I was with My servants Moses and Joshua, so shall I be with you and in you. Turn not away from Me. Give all that you can give. Give the best that you have to give. Expect the best in return.

The Scriptures

The thief cometh not, but for to steal, and to kill, and to destroy: I am come that they might have life, and that they might have it more abundantly.

John 10:10

There shall not any man be able to stand before thee all the days of thy life: as I was with Moses, so I will be with thee: I will not fail thee, nor forsake thee.

Joshua 1:5

Draw nigh to God, and he will draw nigh to you. Cleanse your hands, ye sinners; and purify your hearts, ye double-minded.

James 4:8

O taste and see that the Lord is good: blessed is the man that trusteth in him.

Psalms 34:8

For the Lord God will help me; therefore shall I not be confounded: therefore have I set my face like a flint, and I know that I shall not be ashamed.

Isaiah 50:7

I will lift up mine eyes unto the hills, from whence cometh my help.

My help cometh from the Lord, which made the heaven and earth.

The Lord shall preserve thee from all evil: he shall preserve thy soul.

The Lord shall preserve thy going out and thy coming in from this time forth, and even for evermore.

Psalm 121:1,2,7,8

The Prayer

Father, You are my all. I thank You for salvation. The wells of salvation are dug out and flowing freely in my life; the wells of victory, healing, deliverance, safety, soundness, perseverance, and prosperity. I thank You that You are with me always. The blood of Jesus paid for my life. I surrender it to You. Amen.

Truth Thirty-one

MAGNIFY ME

The Truth

You are an earthen vessel. Magnify Me in your earthen vessel. The world will see Me in You. They will see Me in those who come to know Me because of you. So do not just see your natural face in the mirror, but look into the perfect law of liberty. See My love. Walk in it. Live in it. Show mankind who I am. That is magnification.

The Scriptures

For we preach not ourselves, but Christ Jesus the Lord; and ourselves your servants for Jesus' sake.

For God, who commanded the light to shine out of darkness, hath shined in our hearts, to give the light of the knowledge of the glory of God in the face of Jesus Christ.

But we have this treasure in earthen vessels, that the excellency of the power may be of God, and not of us.

II Corinthians 4:5-7

But be ye doers of the word, and not hearers only, deceiving your own selves.

For if any be a hearer of the word, and not a doer, he is like unto a man beholding his natural face in a glass:

For he beholdeth himself, and goeth his way, and straightway forgetteth what manner of man he was.

But whoso looketh into the perfect law of liberty, and continueth therein, he being not a forgetful hearer, but a doer of the work, this man shall be blessed in his deed.

James 1:22-25

I will bless the Lord at all times: his praise shall continually be in my mouth.

My soul shall make her boast in the Lord: the humble shall hear thereof, and be glad.

O magnify the Lord with me, and let us exalt his name together.

Psalm 34:1-3

For we are his workmanship, created in Christ Jesus unto good works, which God hath before ordained that we should walk in them.

Ephesians 2:10

The Prayer

Father God, I praise You that I am made in Your likeness and in Your image. You formed man from the dust of the earth and breathed into him the breath of life—Your life. You have made me Your righteousness in Christ Jesus. Thank You, Father, for my new life of love, joy, peace, faith, goodness, meekness, longsuffering, temperance and gentleness. May who I am always reflect who You are. Amen.

Truth Thirty-two

SHINE

The Truth

The beauty of a diamond is made perfect when the light shines upon it. The beauty of your life is made perfect when the Light shines through it. Let the Light of who I am be the light of who you are. SHINE!

The Scriptures

Arise, shine; for thy light is come, and the glory of the Lord is risen upon thee.
For, behold, the darkness shall cover the earth, and gross darkness the people: but the Lord shall arise upon thee, and his glory shall be seen upon thee.
Isaiah 60:1, 2

Then shall thy light break forth as the morning, and thine health shall spring forth speedily: and thy righteousness shall go before thee; the glory of the Lord shall be thy rereward.
Isaiah 58:8

THE Lord is my light and my salvation; whom shall I fear? the Lord is the strength of my life; of whom shall I be afraid?
Psalm 27:1

For ye were sometime darkness, but now are ye light in the Lord: walk as children of light:
Ephesians 5:8

But the path of the just is as the shining light, that shineth more and more unto the perfect day.

Proverbs 4:18

For God, who commanded the light to shine out of darkness, hath shined in our hearts, to give the light of the knowledge of the glory of God in the face of Jesus Christ.

II Corinthians 4:6

Then spake Jesus again unto them, saying, I am the light of the world: he that followeth me shall not walk in darkness, but shall have the light of life.

John 8:12

Let your light so shine before men, that they may see your good works, and glorify your Father which is in heaven.

Matthew 5:16

The Prayer

My Lord, My God – both the sun and The Son are Yours. You have given them each for me to enjoy. Thank You for the warmth and the Light as I joy in Your glory. Shine in me and through me! In Christ Jesus, I pray. Amen.

Truth Thirty-three

SET MY AGENDA

The Truth

Prayer in the Spirit before the day's dawning is great and Godly. Prayer shatters and scatters the forces of evil lurking in darkness. These evil forces plot and plan against My children. But, be encouraged. Prayer renders null and void their works and weapons. It renders them harmless and ineffective against a Spirit-led life. Pray early. Pray in the Spirit. Set my agenda. Set your agenda in Me. You cannot afford not to. So Pray!

The Scriptures

I love them that love me; and those that seek me early shall find me.

Proverbs 8:17

GIVE ear to my words, O Lord, consider my meditation.

Hearken unto the voice of my cry, my King, and my God: for unto thee will I pray.

My voice shalt thou hear in the morning, O Lord; in the morning will I direct my prayer unto thee, and will look up.

For thou art not a God that hath pleasure in wickedness: neither shall evil dwell with thee.

The foolish shall not stand in thy sight: thou hatest all workers of iniquity.

Lead me, O Lord in thy righteousness because of mine enemies; make thy way straight before my face.

But let all those that put their trust in thee rejoice: let them ever shout for joy, because thou defendest them: let them also that love thy name be joyful in thee.

Psalm 5:1-5; 8,11

And it shall come to pass, that whosoever shall call on the name of the Lord shall be delivered: for in Mount Zion and in Jerusalem shall be deliverance, as the Lord hath said, and in the remnant whom the Lord shall call.

Joel 2:32

For, behold, the darkness shall cover the earth, and gross darkness the people: but the Lord shall arise upon thee, and his glory shall be seen upon thee.

Isaiah 60:2

Let them be confounded that persecute me, but let not me be confounded: let them be dismayed, but let not me be dismayed: bring upon them the day of evil, and destroy them with double destruction.

Jeremiah 17:18

LET God arise, let his enemies be scattered: let them also that hate him flee before him.

As smoke is driven away, so drive them away: as wax melteth before the fire, so let the wicked perish at the presence of God.

But let the righteous be glad; let them rejoice before God: yea, let them exceedingly rejoice.

Psalm 68:1-3

For I know the thoughts that I think toward you, saith the Lord, thoughts of peace, and not of evil, to give you an expected end.

And ye shall seek me, and find me, when ye shall search for me with all your heart.

Jeremiah 29:11,12

The Prayer

Father, I am safe in Your care. Thank You that I am protected in Your love. You arise and My enemy is scattered. Your Light has come and Your glory is risen upon me. I call upon Your name and I am delivered. Thank You, Father. Amen.

Truth Thirty-four

LIVE THE RESURRECTED LIFE

The Truth

The Word is seed. Jesus is The Word. He died to live again. You, too, must die to live again. Except a seed dies—it cannot live. So die to self and live the resurrected life in Christ.

The Scriptures

IN the beginning was the Word, and the Word was with God, and the Word was God.

John 1:1

Jesus said unto her, I am the resurrection, and the life: he that believeth in me, though he were dead, yet shall he live:

And whosoever liveth and believeth in me shall never die. Believest thou this?

John 11:25,26

I am crucified with Christ: nevertheless I live; yet not I, but Christ liveth in me: and the life which I now live in the flesh I live by the faith of the Son of God, who loved me, and gave himself for me.

Galatians 2:20

But if the Spirit of him that raised up Jesus from the dead dwell in you, he that raised up Christ from the dead shall also quicken your mortal bodies by his Spirit that dwelleth in you.

Romans 8:11

But God, who is rich in mercy, for his great love wherewith he loves us,

Even when we were dead in sins, hath quickened us together with Christ, (by grace ye are saved;)

And hath raised us up together, and made us sit together in heavenly places in Christ Jesus:

Ephesians 2:4-6

The Prayer

Father, I offer my body a living sacrifice, totally and completely to You. Through the Spirit-fill life, I mortify the deeds of my flesh. I am Your disciple. I cast down everything that exalts itself against the knowledge of God. In Your resurrection power I find my dwelling place. Thank You, Father. Amen.

Truth Thirty-five

GIVE

The Truth

Cheerfully give to the Lord all that you are and all that you have. Give so that lives will be changed. Give so that lives will come into the Kingdom. Make a deposit for lost souls. GIVE. Store up an incorruptible treasure as your heavenly reward.

The Scriptures

Every man according as he purposeth in his heart, so let him give; not grudgingly, or of necessity: for God loveth a cheerful giver.

And God is able to make all grace abound toward you; that ye, always having all sufficiency in all things, may abound to every good work:

As it is written, He hath dispersed abroad; he hath given to the poor: his righteousness remaineth forever.

II Corinthians 9:7-9

Lay not up for yourselves treasures upon earth, where moth and rust doth corrupt, and where thieves break through and steal:

But lay up for yourselves treasures in heaven, where neither moth nor rust doth corrupt, and where thieves do not break through nor steal:

For where your treasure is, there will your heart be also.

Matthew 6:19-21

Blessed be the God and Father of our Lord Jesus Christ, which according to his abundant mercy hath begotten us again unto a lively hope by the resurrection of Jesus Christ from the dead,

To an inheritance incorruptible, and undefiled, and that fadeth not away, reserved in heaven for you,

Who are kept by the power of God through faith unto salvation ready to be revealed in the last time.

I Peter 1:3-5

The Prayer

Father, all that is Yours You have given to Jesus. Jesus has given all to me. What I give is not mine, but Yours entrusted through Jesus to me. With a glad heart I give, and great is my reward in heaven. Thank You for every soul that enters into Your Kingdom. Amen.

Truth Thirty-six

YOUR PRAYERS ARE ANSWERED

The Truth

You do not need *special* faith to get answers to your prayers. Hear Me. They are already answered! You just need to speak My word, put your trust in Me and position yourself to receive from Me. It is **My** word that I will bring to pass. The answers will be manifested in your life. The work is already done. I did it for you at Calvary. You must believe. Your prayers are truly answered!

The Scriptures

And Jesus answering saith unto them, Have faith in God.

For verily I say unto you, That whosoever shall say unto this mountain, Be thou removed, and be thou cast into the sea; and shall not doubt in his heart, but shall believe that those things which he saith shall come to pass; he shall have whatsoever he saith.

Therefore I say unto you, What things soever ye desire, when ye pray, believe that ye receive them, and ye shall have them.

Mark 11:22-24

For the Lord God is a sun and shield: the Lord will give grace and glory: no good thing will he withhold from them that walk uprightly.

Psalm 84:11

Call unto me, and I will answer thee, and shew thee great and mighty things, which thou knowest not.

Jeremiah 33:3

So shall my word be that goeth forth out of my mouth: it shall not return unto me void, but it shall accomplish that which I please, and it shall prosper in the thing whereto I sent it.

Isaiah 55:11

The Prayer

Thank You, Father, for Your words which I speak in prayer. Thank You for the measure of faith You have given to me. I trust You to bring into fruition and manifestation in my life those things I have need of. I take no thought for tomorrow. I have no worry for days yet to come. Today I seek Your face. Today I speak Your word. Today I experience Your love. Today I am blessed. In Jesus name. Amen.

Truth Thirty-seven

FOCUS ON JESUS

The Truth

Place a piece of glitter on the floor before you. Fix your eyes upon it and move forward. If you lose sight of the luster, just maintain your focus on that place and keep moving forward. When you reach the spot, the glitter will be there. Focus on Jesus. He is the *glitter* for My Kingdom in the world. Follow Him. Even if you happen to lose sight of Him momentarily, He is always there. He will never leave you, forsake you or fail you. He never changes. He is forever the same. Focus on Him.

The Scriptures

For God so loved the world, that he gave his only begotten Son, that whosoever believeth in him should not perish, but have everlasting life.

John 3:16

Jesus saith unto him, I am the way, the truth, and the life: no man cometh unto the Father, but by me.

John 14:6

Then spake Jesus again unto them, saying, I am the light of the world: he that followeth me shall not walk in darkness, but shall have the light of life.

John 8:12

Jesus Christ the same yesterday, and to-day, and for ever.

Hebrews 13:8

Be ye therefore followers of God, as dear children;
Ephesians 5:1

The Prayer

Thank You, Father, for giving Jesus as the light to a dark and dying world. He is that light which shines out of darkness. He is life to those who find Him. He is the lamp unto my feet and the light unto my path. I will keep my focus on Him. I will always do the things which please my Lord and Savior. Amen.

Truth Thirty-eight

BEAR FRUIT

The Truth

I am the vine. You are the branch. Stay connected to Me. Bear fruit. Take the spiritual fruit that you bear and give it to another. Empty your supply that I might replenish it. As you give, you grow. As you grow, you bear more fruit to share with others so that they too, will grow.

The Scriptures

The fruit of the righteous is a tree of life; and he that winneth souls is wise.

Proverbs 11:30

I the Lord search the heart, I try the reins, even to give every man according to his ways, and according to the fruit of his doings.

Jeremiah 17:10

But the fruit of the Spirit is love, joy, peace, longsuffering, gentleness, goodness, faith, Meekness, temperance: against such there is no law.

Galatians 5:22,23

But he that received seed into the good ground is he that heareth the word, and understandeth it; which also beareth fruit, and bringeth forth, some an hundredfold, some sixty, some thirty.

Matthew 13:23

But seek ye first the kingdom of God, and his righteousness; and all these things shall be added unto you.
Matthew 6:33

*Verily, verily, I say unto you, Except a corn of wheat fall into the ground and die, it abideth alone: but if it die, **it bringeth forth much fruit.** (Authors' emphasis in bold)*
John 12:24

A man shall be satisfied with good by the fruit of his mouth:
Proverbs 12:14a

The Prayer

I thank You for the fruit of the Spirit that You manifest in my life. I want to share Your love and goodness with others. Help me to give always. I will stay connected to You and sow seeds of love and kindness that produce harvests of souls for Your Kingdom. In the name of Jesus. Amen.

Truth Thirty-nine

SPEAK MY WORD

The Truth

The seed in you is the product of your spoken words, your prayers, your praise, and your worship. My word is near you, even in your mouth. Speak My word. Your harvest reaped is in proportion to your seed sown. Sow for a bountiful harvest.

The Scriptures

And he said unto them, Take heed what ye hear: With what measure ye mete, it shall be measured to you: and unto you that hear shall more be given.

Mark 4:24

Give, and it shall be given unto you; good measure, pressed down, and shaken together, and running over, shall men give into your bosom. For with the same measure that ye mete withal it shall be measured to you again.

Luke 6:38

But what saith it? The word is nigh thee, even in thy mouth, and in thy heart: that is, the word of faith, which we preach;

Romans 10:8

The Prayer

O for a thousand tongues to sing Your praises, My Lord, Most High. Your words will I hide in my heart. I know that they are powerful and alive. I will partake of them every day. I will offer praises and thanksgiving from a pure heart. I will be still and see Your salvation. In Christ Jesus I pray. Amen.

Truth Forty

STAY IN ME

The Truth

The storms of life will come. The winds will blow and the rains will pour. Through it all, beyond it all, after it all, above it all, in it all, I am your protector.

As with Daniel, I am your lion tamer. As with Shadrach, Meshach and Abednego, I am your fourth man in the fire. As with David, I am your shepherd. As with Elijah, I am your cloud like a man's hand. As with Stephen, I am standing at the right hand of the Father for you. I can still every storm. Stay in me.

Stay with me.

The Scriptures

Then the king commanded, and they brought Daniel, and cast him into the den of lions. Now the king spake and said unto Daniel, Thy God whom thou servest continually, he will deliver thee.

Daniel 6:16

My God hath sent his angel, and hath shut the lions' mouths, that they have not hurt me:

forasmuch as before him innocency was found in me; and also before thee, O king, have I done no hurt.

Daniel 6:22

If it be so, our God whom we serve is able to deliver us from the burning fiery furnace, and he will deliver us out of thine hand, O king.

Daniel 3:17

He answered and said, Lo, I see four men loose, walking in the midst of the fire, and they have no hurt; and the form of the fourth is like the Son of God.

Daniel 3:25

THE Lord is my shepherd; I shall not want.

Psalm 23:1

And said, Behold, I see the heavens opened, and the Son of man standing on the right hand of God.

Acts 7:56

And he saith unto them, Why are ye fearful, O ye of little faith? Then he arose, and rebuked the winds and the sea; and there was a great calm.

Matthew 8:26

The Prayer

Thank You, Father, that You are a present help in time of trouble. You are my rock, my fortress, my shield, my buckler and my strength. I am hidden under the pavilion of Your love. Thank You for keeping me safe and secure. Thank You for hearing and answering prayer. In the name of Jesus I pray. Amen.

Truth Forty-one

KNOW THAT I AM GOD

The Truth

Satan goes about as a roaring lion seeking whom he may devour. You are hidden and protected in Christ. Remember the childhood days of hide-and-seek? Your strategy was to be still, stand firm and fully expect the "seeker" to pass you by. Good strategy! Use it now. Be still. Know that I am God.

The Scriptures

My Father, which gave them me, is greater than all; and no man is able to pluck them out of my Father's hand.

John 10:29

Be sober, be vigilant; because your adversary the devil, as a roaring lion, walketh about, seeking whom he may devour:

I Peter 5:8

Be still, and know that I am God: I will be exalted among the heathen, I will be exalted in the earth.

Psalms 46:10

For the which cause I also suffer these things: nevertheless I am not ashamed: for I know whom I have believed, and am persuaded that he is able to keep that which I have committed unto him against that day.

II Timothy 1:12

The Prayer

Thank You, Father, that in Jesus I am safe, sane, saved, sensible, sound, sober, strong, secure, settled, sanctified, satisfied and serving You today and all of my tomorrows. I have a shout in my heart. It says, HALLELUJAH! Amen.

Truth Forty-two

DO NOT MURMUR OR COMPLAIN

The Truth

In prayer, speak the answer from God's word to the situation around you or the condition within you. Forsake murmuring and complaining. Do not speak the situation or condition as you see it. Speak My word. My word will bring forth the manifestation that you are seeking in your life. My word will not return empty. Understand this. Christ, the Anointed One, is in you.

The Scriptures

Cast not away therefore your confidence, which hath great recompense of reward.

For ye have need of patience, that, after ye have done the will of God, ye might receive the promise.

Hebrews 10:35,36

But as we were allowed of God to be put in trust with the gospel, even so we speak; not as pleasing men, but God, which trieth our hearts.

I Thessalonians 2:4

My son, attend to my words; incline thine ear unto my sayings.

Let them not depart from thine eyes; keep them in the midst of thine heart.

For they are life unto those that find them, and health to all their flesh.

Proverbs 4:20-22

So shall my word be that goeth forth out of my mouth: it shall not return unto me void, but it shall accomplish that which I please, and it shall prosper in the thing whereto I sent it.

Isaiah 55:11

The Prayer

Thank You, Father, that You have given to me everything that pertains to life and godliness. Thank You for blessing me with every spiritual blessing in heavenly places. My confidence is in You. You withhold no good thing from me. There is no shadow of turning with You. If I ask anything in Your name, You promise to do it. Thank You for hearing my prayers. Thank You for revealing Yourself to me. Thank You for showing me great and mighty things. I love You and I keep Your commandments. Amen.

Truth Forty-three

REST IN ME

The Truth

It should bring comfort to you to know that I love you and I am always with you. Think of the true earthly friends you have in whose company you can rest, relax, and have peace. Now, think of the true Heavenly Friend you have. In My presence you can rest, relax and have peace that passes all understanding. Come. Abide in me. Rest in me.

The Scriptures

Return unto thy rest, O my soul; for the Lord hath dealt bountifully with thee.

Psalm 116:7

If ye love me, keep my commandments.
And I will pray the Father, and he shall give you another Comforter, that he may abide with you for ever;

John 14:15,16

I will not leave you comfortless: I will come to you.

John 14:18

Greater love hath no man than this, that a man lay down his life for his friends.
Ye are my friends, if ye do whatsoever I command you.
Henceforth I call you not servants; for the servant knoweth not what his lord doeth: but I have called you

friends; for all things that I have heard of my Father I have made known to you.

John 15:13-15

The Prayer

Thank You, Father, for the friends You have given in the earth to share in my life and me in theirs. Thank You even more for Jesus; the greatest Friend of all. Jesus laid down His life for me. He took my sin so that I can have His life. He is my life. He is my peace. I abide in His love. I find rest in Him. I am an heir of salvation. Thank You for giving me Jesus. Amen.

Truth Forty-four

FEAR NOT

The Truth

David, the shepherd boy, said he would kill the giant in his day. He was no match for the Philistine giant, but he claimed victory over him. He planned his course of action. He was submitted to the Lord God of Israel. He chose his weapon, ran into the enemy's territory and executed his plan even as he said. David refused to allow the enemy to put fear in his heart. You go and do likewise. Fear not! I am your God. I am with you.

The Scriptures

Then said David to the Philistine, Thou comest to me with a sword, and with a spear, and with a shield: but I come to thee in the name of the Lord of hosts, the God of the armies of Israel, whom thou hast defied.

And all this assembly shall know that the Lord saveth not with sword and spear: for the battle is the Lord's, and he will give you into our hands.

So David prevailed over the Philistine with a sling and with a stone, and smote the Philistine, and slew him; but there was no sword in the hand of David.

I Samuel 17:45,47,50

Fear thou not; for I am with thee: be not dismayed; for I am thy God: I will strengthen thee; yea, I will help thee: ye, I will uphold thee with the right hand of my righteousness.

Isaiah 41:10

For God hath not given us the spirit of fear; but of power, and of love, and of a sound mind.

II Timothy 1:7

That at the name of Jesus every knee should bow, of things in heaven, and things in earth, and things under the earth;

Philippians 2:10

The Prayer

Dear Lord, I will not be fearful or troubled. You have not given me a spirit of fear, but of power, love, and soundness of mind. I draw near to You. I resist the enemy and he must flee from me. You have made him my footstool. Thank You, Father, for this authority and power over my enemy. Thank You for the blood of Jesus. Thank You for the name of Jesus. Amen.

Truth Forty-five

OPEN THE DOOR OF FAITH

The Truth

Open the door of faith with your prayers. Believe My word in your heart and speak it with your mouth. Stand on the authority of My word and the power therein. Rejoice as you stand. Seek Me. Trust Me. See the glory of your Lord.

The Scriptures

But without faith it is impossible to please him; for he that cometh to God must believe that he is, and that he is a rewarder of them that diligently seek him.

Hebrews 11:6

And ye shall seek me, and find me, when you shall search for me with all your heart.

Jeremiah 29:13

Seek ye the Lord while he may be found, call ye upon him while he is near:

Isaiah 55:6

Then shall ye call upon me, and ye shall go and pray unto me, and I will hearken unto you.

Jeremiah 29:12

Stand therefore, having your loins girt about with truth, and having on the breastplate of righteousness;

And your feet shod with the preparation of the gospel of peace;

Ephesians 6:14,15

In everything give thanks: for this is the will of God in Christ Jesus concerning you.

I Thessalonians 5:18

Jesus saith unto her, Said I not unto thee, that, if thou wouldest believe, thou shouldest see the glory of God?

John 11:40

The Prayer

According to Your word, O Lord, Your glory and Your promises are mine. All that You have is mine. Hear my prayer and answer according to Your loving kindness. I am empowered to prosper in every area of my being. I abide in Your word. I am Your abiding place, the temple of Your Holy Spirit. Show me Your glory. In the name of Jesus, our Lord. Amen.

Truth Forty-six

LIVE HOLY

The Truth

I am calling you, My church, back to prayer. I want to make deposits into each of your lives and into My church. I am looking for a church without spot or blemish. I am revealing and unveiling in the lives and circumstances of My people. I am *weeding out* those who are not sacrificed and committed to My plans and purposes. It is time for holiness. Live Holy.

The Scriptures

Therefore judge nothing before the time, until the Lord come, who both will bring to light the hidden things of darkness, and will make manifest the counsels of the hearts: and then shall every man have praise of God.

I Corinthians 4:5

For there is nothing covered, that shall not be revealed; neither hid, that shall not be known.

Luke 12:2

I BESEECH you therefore, brethren, by the mercies of God, that ye present your bodies a living sacrifice, holy, acceptable unto God, which is your reasonable service.

Romans 12:1

I speak after the manner of men because of the infirmity of your flesh: for as ye have yielded your members servants to uncleanness and to iniquity unto iniquity; even so now yield your members servants to righteousness unto holiness.

Romans 6:19

But ye are a chosen generation, a royal priesthood, an holy nation, a peculiar people; that ye should shew forth the praises of him who hath called you out of darkness into his marvellous light:

I Peter 2:9

HAVING therefore these promises, dearly beloved, let us cleanse ourselves from all filthiness of the flesh and spirit, perfecting holiness in the fear of God.

II Corinthians 7:1

Commit thy way unto the Lord; trust also in him; and he shall bring it to pass.

Psalm 37:5

That he might present it to himself a glorious church, not having spot, or wrinkle, or any such thing; but that it should be holy and without blemish.

Ephesians 5:27

The Prayer

I am grateful, Father, for fellowship and intimacy with You. Thank You for the privilege of prayer; for inviting me into Your throne room. You are holy. I offer myself a living sacrifice to You, so that I may be holy. I am washed, cleansed, purified and sanctified in You. By Your grace and mercy, I walk perfect and upright in Jesus my Lord. Amen.

Truth Forty-seven

YOU ARE MINE

The Truth

You are an overcomer. You are Mine. You are more than a conqueror in Christ Jesus. Nothing and no one can by any means pluck you out of My hands. You are Mine.

The Scriptures

BUT now thus saith the lord that created thee, O Jacob, and he that formed thee, O Israel, Fear not: for I have redeemed thee, I have called thee by thy name; thou are mine.

Isaiah 43:1

I have manifested thy name unto the men which thou gavest me out of the world: thine they were, and thou gavest them me; and they have kept my word.

I pray for them: I pray not for the world, but for them which thou hast given me; for they are thine.

And all mine are thine, and thine are mine; and I am glorified in them.

John 17:6,9,10

My Father, which gave them me, is greater than all; and no man is able to pluck them out of my Father's hand.

John 10:29

Ye are of God, little children, and have overcome them: because greater is he that is in you, than he that is in the world.

I John 4:4

And they overcame him by the blood of the Lamb, and by the word of their testimony; and they loved not their lives unto the death.

Revelation 12:11

To him that overcometh will I grant to sit with me in my throne, even as I also overcame, and am set down with my Father in his throne.

Revelation 3:21

…in all these things we are more than conquerors through him that loved us.

Romans 8: 37b

The Prayer

Thank You, Father, that the battle is Yours—the victory is mine. Thank You, that I have made You, the Most High, my dwelling place. No evil has victory over me. No curse overshadows me. Angels watch over me. I am safe in Your hands. I am Yours. I live to serve You. May my life always be a living testimony of Your love and mercy. Amen

Truth Forty-eight

YOU ARE MY TEMPLE

The Truth

After you have done all you can do, stand. Stand in the midst of the trial or test. You are my temple. Be still and see My presence and power as I rise up on the inside of you by My Spirit and anoint you with My glory. Then your test will become a testimony of My saving grace.

The Scriptures

Know ye not that ye are the temple of God, and that the Spirit of God dwelleth in you?

I Corinthians 3:16

Even the Spirit of truth; whom the world cannot receive, because it seeth him not, neither knoweth him: but ye know him; for he dwelleth with you, and shall be in you.

John 14:17

My brethren, count it all joy when ye fall into divers temptations;

Knowing this, that the trying of your faith worketh patience.

James 1:2,3

Beloved, think it not strange concerning the fiery trial which is to try you, as though some strange thing happened unto you:

But rejoice, inasmuch as ye are partakers of Christ's sufferings; that, when his glory shall be revealed, ye may be glad also with exceeding joy.

I Peter 4:12,13

Blessed is the man that endureth temptation: for when he is tried, he shall receive the crown of life, which the Lord hath promised to them that love him.

James 1:12

Put on the whole armour of God, that ye may be able to stand against the wiles of the devil.

Ephesians 6:11

These things I have spoken unto you, that in me ye might have peace. In the world ye shall have tribulation: but be of good cheer; I have overcome the world.

John 16:33

Now the God of hope fill you with all joy and peace in believing, that ye may abound in hope, through the power of the Holy Ghost.

Romans 15:13

The Prayer

Father, I know that You love me. Thank You for saving me and giving to me the strength to stand when standing is all I can do. Thank You for Your grace which is sufficient for me. Thank You for Your truth which makes me free. As You rise up in me to show Yourself strong on my behalf, I yield my will to Your will. Thank You for the anointing of Your glory - Your presence – Your power - in me. In the name of Jesus Christ I pray. Amen.

Truth Forty-nine

YOU ARE NOT ALONE

The Truth

Always remember that I am with you. I never leave you. I never abandon you. I cannot fail you. You are never alone. Nothing can separate you from My love. Nothing! Trust Me <u>with</u> everything. Trust Me <u>for</u> everything. Trust Me <u>in</u> everything.

The Scriptures

When thou passest through the waters, I will be with thee; and through the rivers, they shall not overflow thee: when thou walkest through the fire, thou shalt not be burned; neither shall the flame kindle upon thee.

Isaiah 43:2

Who shall separate us from the love of Christ? Shall tribulation, or distress, or persecution, or famine, or nakedness, or peril, or sword?

As it is written, For thy sake we are killed all the day long; we are accounted as sheep for the slaughter.

Nay, in all these things we are more than conquerors through him that loved us.

For I am persuaded, that neither death, nor life, nor angels, nor principalities, nor powers, nor things present, nor things to come,

Nor height, nor depth, nor any other creature, shall be able to separate us from the love of God, which is in Christ Jesus our Lord.

Romans 8:35-39

Though I walk in the midst of trouble, thou wilt revive me: thou shalt stretch forth thine hand against the wrath of mine enemies, and thy right hand shall save me.

Psalm 138:7

The Lord is my rock, and my fortress, and my deliverer; my God, my strength, in whom I will trust; my buckler, and the horn of my salvation, and my high tower.

Psalm 18:2

The Lord is good, a strong hold in the day of trouble: and he knoweth them that trust in him.

Nahum 1:7

For the Lord God is a sun and shield: the Lord will give grace and glory: no good thing will he withhold from them that walk uprightly.

O Lord of hosts, blessed is the man that trusteth in thee.

Psalm 84:11,12

...and, lo, I am with you alway, even unto the end of the world. Amen.

Matthew 28:20b

The Prayer

Father, I thank You for the assurance in Your word that You are always with me. Thank You that You never abandon me and I am never outside of Your love. May I always trust You for everything. May I always trust You in everything. May I always trust You

with everything. Now and forever, my hope is in You.
Amen.

Truth Fifty

FORGIVE AND BE FREE

The Truth

Forgive. You must forgive! An unforgiving heart causes you, My dear child, physical, emotional and spiritual damage. You cannot hold on to the wrongs, hurts or injustices caused you by another and be free. Those same wrongs, hurts and injustices are also holding on to you. Release them so that they can release you. Forgive and be forgiven. Cast your cares upon Me. BE FREE.

The Scriptures

FRET not thyself because of evildoers, neither be thou envious against the workers of iniquity.

For they shall soon be cut down like the grass, and wither as the green herb.

Psalm 37:1,2

But I say unto you, Love your enemies, bless them that curse you, do good to them that hate you, and pray for them which despitefully use you, and persecute you;

That ye may be the children of your Father which is in heaven:

Matthew 5:44,45a

Be ye therefore merciful, as your Father also is merciful.

Judge not, and ye shall not be judged: condemn not, and ye shall not be condemned: forgive, and ye shall be forgiven:

Luke 6:36,37

Forbearing one another, and forgiving one another, if any man have a quarrel against any: even as Christ forgave you, so also do ye.

Colossians 3:13

And when you stand praying, forgive, if ye have aught against any: that your Father also which is in heaven may forgive you your trespasses.

But if ye do not forgive, neither will your Father which is in heaven forgive your trespasses.

Mark 11:25,26

If I regard iniquity in my heart, the Lord will not hear me:

Psalm 66:18

WHEREFORE seeing we also are compassed about with so great a cloud of witnesses, let us lay aside every weight, and the sin which doth so easily beset us, and let us run with patience the race that is set before us,

Looking unto Jesus the author and finisher of our faith; who for the joy that was set before him endured the cross, despising the shame, and is set down at the right hand of the throne of God.

For consider him that endured such contradiction of sinners against himself, lest ye be wearied and faint in your minds.

Hebrews 12:1-3

Casting all your care upon him; for he careth for you.
I Peter 5:7

The Prayer

Father, thank You for forgiving me as I readily and willingly forgive others. I cast every care upon You. I release all wrongs, hurts and injustices done against me and I receive the joy of Your healing love as it flows through me. I thank You that I am free. In Jesus name. Amen.

Truth Fifty-one

LIVE BY FAITH

The Truth

Your faith is alive. Your faith teaches. Your faith talks. Your faith stands. Your faith walks. Your faith is great. Your faith is strong. Please Me. Live by faith!

The Scriptures

But that no man is justified by the law in the sight of God, it is evident: for, The just shall live by faith.

Galatians 3:11

This only would I learn of you, Received ye the Spirit by the works of the law, or by the hearing of faith?

Galatians 3:2

Not for that we have dominion over your faith, but are helpers of your joy: for by faith ye stand.

II Corinthians 1:24

For we walk by faith, not by sight:

II Corinthians 5:7

When Jesus heard it, he marvelled, and said to them that followed, Verily I say unto you, I have not found so great faith, no, not in Israel.

Matthew 8:10

And being not weak in faith, he considered not his own body now dead, when he was about a hundred years old, neither yet the deadness of Sarah's womb:

*He staggered not at the promise of God through unbelief;
but was strong in faith, giving glory to God;*

Romans 4:19,20

The Prayer

Thank You, Father, for the measure of faith. When I come to a mountain of life, I will speak. When the enemy comes, I will resist. I will call out to You as I seek Your Kingdom above all else. I will walk across every Red Sea or Jordan River or around every Jericho Wall which may present itself as an adverse circumstance in my life. After I have done all to stand, I will stand strong in my Lord Jesus. In faith, I will be standing when You return to take me home. GLORY!

Truth Fifty-two

GUARD YOUR MOUTH

The Truth

The thing which is dictated to your life from the sources, situations and circumstances around you begins in the mind. Think before you receive it. Next, it drops into the spirit. Think before you conceive it. Judge it. Is it good? Is it acceptable? Is it perfect? Should it be kept? Should it be cast down? Once believed in the heart and spoken out of the mouth, it is destined to shape your future. Live wisely. Guard your mouth! Watch your words. Make them Mine.

The Scriptures

He that keepeth his mouth keepeth his life: but he that openeth wide his lips shall have destruction.

Proverbs 13:3

Let this mind be in you, which was also in Christ Jesus:

Philippians 2:5

And be not conformed to this world: but be ye transformed by the renewing of your mind, that ye may prove what is that good, and acceptable, and perfect, will of God.

Romans 12:2

Casting down imaginations, and every high thing that exalteth itself against the knowledge of God, and bringing into captivity every thought to the obedience of Christ;

And having in a readiness to revenge all disobedience, when your obedience is fulfilled.

II Corinthians 10:5,6

Set a watch, O Lord, before my mouth; keep the door of my lips.

Psalm 141:3

Thou art snared with the words of thy mouth, thou art taken with the words of thy mouth.

Proverbs 6:2

...for out of the abundance of the heart the mouth speaketh.

A good man out of the good treasure of the heart bringeth forth good things: and an evil man out of the evil treasure bringeth forth evil things.

But I say unto you, That every idle word that men shall speak, they shall give account thereof in the day of judgment.

For by thy words thou shalt be justified, and by thy words thou shalt be condemned.

Matthew 12:34b-37

But what saith it? The word is nigh thee, even in thy mouth, and in thy heart: that is, the word of faith, which we preach;

Romans 10:8

Bind them continually upon thine heart, and tie them about thy neck.

When thou goest, it shall lead thee; when thou sleepest, it shall keep thee; and when thou awakest, it shall talk with thee.

Proverbs 6:21,22

My son, attend to my words; incline thine ear unto my sayings.

Let them not depart from thine eyes; keep them in the midst of thine heart.

For they are life unto those that find them, and health to all their flesh.

Keep thy heart with all diligence; for out of it are the issues of life.

Put away from thee a froward mouth, and perverse lips put far from thee.

Turn not to the right hand nor to the left: remove thy foot from evil.

Proverbs 4:20-24, 27

The Prayer

Father, I hide Your word in my heart so that I will not sin against You; so that in me there will be no guile; so that I will be a follower of Christ; so that I will say those things I hear You say; and so that I will do those things I see You do. Let not the thoughts of my enemy, become my own. Let not the weapons he forms prosper against me. I am Your righteousness in Christ Jesus, my King. Today I speak all of my tomorrows into days of Kingdom living. In Jesus Name, Amen.

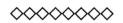

NOW UNTO HIM
THAT IS ABLE TO DO
EXCEEDING
ABUNDANTLY ABOVE
ALL THAT WE ASK OR
THINK, ACCORDING
TO THE POWER
THAT WORKETH IN
US, UNTO HIM BE
GLORY
IN THE CHURCH
BY CHRIST JESUS
THROUGHOUT
ALL AGES, WORLD
WITHOUT END.
AMEN.

EPHESIANS 3:20,21

PART III
KINGDOM
PROMISES

*Enlightenment and
fulfillment in
Kingdom living.*

Introduction to Kingdom Promises

God has given us all things that pertain to life and godliness. If our prayer life is not fruitful, we should go back to God and *reason together* with Him. God is God. He changes not. He will make us the children He desires us to be if we align ourselves with Him and His eternal plan. His making of us does not imply a forcing upon us of His will, but rather His transforming work which we allow to take place within us. He is Savior, Lord, and King in our lives only to the extent and degree that we choose.

The clay cannot shape itself, but the Potter can and will. The Potter, our Master, will make us vessels of honor as we submit to the work of His hands. This submission calls for the death of our carnal thought life to be replaced with a mind renewed to the word of God. His work will draw us to Him until His will becomes our own. Then, we will see the promises of God manifested in our lives by the Holy Spirit. We will begin to resemble Him in every way.

The Bible tells us in Numbers 23:19 that God is not a man that He should lie. What He has promised, He will make happen. His promises are His words and He watches over His words to perform them.

My covenant will I not break, nor alter the thing that is gone out of my lips.

Psalm 89:34

For as the rain cometh down, and the snow from the heaven, and returneth not thither, but watereth the earth, and maketh it bring forth and bud, that it may give seed to the sower, and bread to the eater:

So shall my word be that goeth forth out of my mouth: it shall not return unto me void, but it shall accomplish that which I please, and it shall prosper in the thing whereto I sent it.

Isaiah 55:10,11

When we establish hope in His words, He sees our thoughts. When we confess His words in faith, He sees our hearts. When we pray according to His word (which is His will), He brings it to pass. There are many scriptures in the Bible representing Kingdom promises and abundance. Here are but a few of them. Know that God can and will supply your every need.

Names of Promises

Peace

Safety

Soundness

Healing

Grace

Love

Prosperity

Prayer

Mercy

Deliverance

Victory

Perseverance

PEACE

The Lord will give strength unto his people; the Lord will bless his people with peace.

Psalm 29:11

For he is our peace, who hath made both one, and hath broken down the middle wall of partition between us;

Ephesians 2:14

Thou wilt keep him in perfect peace, whose mind is stayed on thee: because he trusteth in thee.

Isaiah 26:3

Lord, thou wilt ordain peace for us: for thou also hast wrought all our works in us.

Isaiah 26.12

And let the peace of God rule in your hearts, to the which also ye are called in one body; and be ye thankful.

Colossians 3:15

THEREFORE being justified by faith, we have peace with God through our Lord Jesus Christ:

Romans 5:1

Peace I leave with you, my peace I give unto you: not as the world giveth, give I unto you. Let not your heart be troubled, neither let it be afraid.

John 14:27

Be careful for nothing; but in everything by prayer and supplication with thanksgiving let your requests be made known unto God.

And the peace of God, which passeth all understanding, shall keep your hearts and minds through Christ Jesus.

Those things, which ye have both learned, and received, and heard, and seen in me, do: and the God of peace shall be with you.

Philippians 4:6,7,9

Finally, brethren, farewell. Be perfect, be of good comfort, be of one mind, live in peace; and the God of love and peace shall be with you.

II Corinthians 13:11

SAFETY

Blessed be the God and Father of our Lord Jesus Christ, which according to his abundant mercy hath begotten us again unto a lively hope by the resurrection of Jesus Christ from the dead,

To an inheritance incorruptible, and undefiled, and that fadeth not away, reserved in heaven for you,

Who are kept by the power of God through faith unto salvation ready to be revealed in the last time.

I Peter 3-5

But the Lord is faithful, who shall stablish you, and keep you from evil.

II Thessalonians 3:3

Surely goodness and mercy shall follow me all the days of my life: and I will dwell in the house of the Lord for ever.

Psalm 23:6

Who hath also sealed us, and given the earnest of the Spirit in our hearts.

II Corinthians 1:22

Being confident of this very thing, that he which hath begun a good work in you will perform it until the day of Jesus Christ:

Philippians 1:6

My sheep hear my voice, and I know them, and they follow me:

155

And I give unto them eternal life; and they shall never perish, neither shall any man pluck them out of my hand.

John 10:27,28

And grieve not the holy Spirit of God, whereby ye are sealed unto the day of redemption.

Ephesians 4:30

I will both lay me down in peace, and sleep: for thou, Lord, only makest me dwell in safety.

Psalm 4:8

HE that dwelleth in the secret place of the most High shall abide under the shadow of the Almighty.

I will say of the Lord, He is my refuge and my fortress: my God; in him will I trust.

Surely he shall deliver thee from the snare of the fowler, and from the noisome pestilence.

Thou shalt not be afraid for the terror by night; nor for the arrow that flieth by day;

Nor for the pestilence that walketh in darkness; nor for the destruction that wasteth at noonday.

A thousand shall fall at thy side, and ten thousand at thy right hand; but it shall not come nigh thee.

Only with thine eyes shalt thou behold and see the reward of the wicked.

Because thou hast made the Lord, which is my refuge, even the most High, thy habitation;

There shall no evil befall thee, neither shall any plague come nigh thy dwelling.

For he shall give his angels charge over thee, to keep thee in all thy ways.

Psalm 91:1-11

For in the time of trouble he shall hide me in his pavilion: in the secret of his tabernacle shall he hide me; he shall set me up upon a rock.

And now shall mine head be lifted up about mine enemies round about me:

Psalm 27:5,6a

SOUNDNESS

Be careful for nothing; but in every thing by prayer and supplication with thanksgiving let your request be made known unto God.

And the peace of God, which passeth all understanding, shall keep your hearts and minds through Christ Jesus.

Finally, brethren, whatsoever things are true, whatsoever things are honest, whatsoever things are just, whatsoever things are pure, whatsoever things are of good report; if there be any virtue, and if there be any praise, think on these things.

Philippians 4:6-8

Peace I leave with you, my peace I give unto you: not as the world giveth, give I unto you. Let not your heart be troubled, neither let it be afraid.

John 14:27

For to be carnally minded is death; but to be spiritually minded is life and peace.

Romans 8:6

Let not your heart be troubled: ye believe in God, believe also in me.

John 14:1

Be of good courage, and he shall strengthen your heart, all ye that hope in the Lord.

Psalm 31:24

Ye are of God, little children, and have overcome them: because greater is he that is in you, than he that is in the world.

I John 4:4

Thou wilt keep him in perfect peace, whose mind is stayed on thee: because he trusteth in thee.

Isaiah 26:3

And let the peace of God rule in your hearts, to the which also ye are called in one body; and be ye thankful.

Colossians 3:15

And be not conformed to this world: but be ye transformed by the renewing of your mind, that ye may prove what is that good, and acceptable, and perfect, will of God.

Romans 12:2

For who hath known the mind of the Lord, that he may instruct him? But we have the mind of Christ.

I Corinthians 2:16

Let this mind be in you, which was also in Christ Jesus:

Philippians 2:5

For God hath not given us a spirit of fear; but of power, and of love, and of a sound mind.

I Timothy 1:7

Hold fast the form of sound words, which thou hast heard of me, in faith and love which is in Christ Jesus.

I Timothy 1:13

As ye have therefore received Christ Jesus the Lord, so walk in him:

Rooted and built up in him, and stablished in faith, as ye have been taught, abounding therein with thanksgiving.

Colossians 2:6,7

But we have this treasure in earthen vessels, that the excellency of the power may be of God, and not of us.

II Corinthians 4:7

Consider what I say; and the Lord give thee understanding in all things.

II Timothy 2:7

But continue thou in the things which thou hast learned and hast been assured of, knowing of whom thou hast learned them;

And that from a child thou hast known the holy scriptures, which are able to make thee wise unto salvation though faith which is in Christ Jesus.

II Timothy 3:14,15

HEALING

And the whole multitude sought to touch him: for there went virtue out of him, and healed them all.

Luke 6:19

For I will restore health unto thee, and I will heal thee of thy wounds, saith the Lord;

Jeremiah 20:17a

Who his own self bare our sins in his own body on the tree, that we, being dead to sins, should live unto righteousness: by whose stripes ye were healed.

I Peter 2:24

And Jesus went about all the cities and villages, teaching in their synagogues, and preaching the gospel of the kingdom, and healing every sickness and every disease among the people.

Matthew 9:35

Beloved, I wish above all things that thou mayest prosper and be in health, even as thy soul prospereth.

III John 2

Heal me, O Lord, and I shall be healed; save me, and I shall be saved: for thou art my praise.

Jeremiah 17:14

But he was wounded for our transgressions, he was bruised for our iniquities: the chastisement of our peace was upon him; and with his stripes we are healed.

Isaiah 53:5

...If thou wilt diligently hearken to the voice of the Lord thy God, and wilt do that which is right in his sight, and wilt give ear to his commandments, and keep all his statutes, I will put none of these diseases upon thee, which I have brought upon the Egyptians: for I am the Lord that healeth thee.

Exodus 15:26

He sent his word, and healed them, and delivered them from their destructions.

Psalm 107:20

Is any sick among you? Let him call for the elders of the church; and let them pray over him, anointing him with oil in the name of the Lord:

And the prayer of faith shall save the sick, and the Lord shall raise him up; and if he have committed sins, they shall be forgiven him.

James 5:14,15

And these signs shall follow them that believe; In my name shall they cast out devils; they shall speak with new tongues;

They shall take up serpents; and if they drink any deadly thing, it shall not hurt them; they shall lay hands on the sick, and they shall recover.

Mark 16:17,18

GRACE

For by grace are ye saved through faith; and that not of yourselves: it is the gift of God:

Not of works, lest any man should boast.

Ephesians 1:8,9

For the law was given by Moses, but grace and truth came by Jesus Christ.

John 1:17

For all have sinned, and come short of the glory of God;

Being justified freely by his grace through the redemption that is in Christ Jesus:

Romans 3:23,24

But not as the offence, so also is the free gift. For if through the offence of one many be dead, much more the grace of God, and the gift by grace, which is by one man, Jesus Christ, hath abounded unto many.

For if by one man's offence death reigned by one; much more they which receive abundance of grace and of the gift of righteousness shall reign in life by one, Jesus Christ.

That as sin hath reigned unto death, even so might grace reign through righteousness unto eternal life by Jesus Christ our Lord.

Romans 5:15,17, 21

For sin shall not have dominion over you: for ye are not under the law, but under grace.

What then? Shall we sin, because we are not under the law, but under grace? God forbid.

Romans 6:14,15

But by the grace of God I am what I am: and his grace which was bestowed upon me was not in vain; but I laboured more abundantly than they all: yet not I, but the grace of God which was with me.

I Corinthians 15:10

WE then, as workers together with him, beseech you also that ye receive not the grace of God in vain.

II Corinthians 6:1

And God is able to make all grace abound toward you; that ye, always having all sufficiency in all things, may abound to every good work:

II Corinthians 9:8

And he said unto me, My grace is sufficient for thee: for my strength is made perfect in weakness.

II Corinthians 12:9a

But God, who is rich in mercy, for his great love wherewith he loved us,

Even when we were dead in sins, hath quickened us together with Christ, (by grace ye are saved;)

And hath raised us up together, and made us sit together in heavenly places in Christ Jesus.

That in the ages to come he might shew the exceeding riches of his grace in his kindness toward us through Christ Jesus.

Ephesians 2:4-7

But unto every one of us is given grace according to the measure of the gift of Christ.

Ephesians 4:7

LOVE

For God so loved the world, that he gave his only begotten Son, that whosoever believeth in him should not perish, but have everlasting life.

John 3:16

The Lord hath appeared of old unto me, saying, Yea, I have loved thee with an everlasting love: therefore with lovingkindness have I drawn thee.

Jeremiah 31:3

And we have known and believed the love that God hath to us. God is love; and he that dwelleth in love dwelleth in God, and God in him.

I John 4:16

I love them that love me; and those that seek me early shall find me.

Proverbs 8:17

But as it is written, Eye hath not seen, nor ear heard, neither have entered into the heart of man, the things which God hath prepared for them that love him.

I Corinthians 2:9

Herein is love, not that we loved God, but that he loved us, and sent his Son to be the propitiation for our sins.

I John 4:10

He that hath my commandments, and keepeth them, he it is that loveth me: and he that loveth me shall be loved of my Father, and I will love him, and will manifest myself to him.

John 14:21

The Lord preserveth all them that love him: but all the wicked will he destroy.

Psalm 145:20

…If a man love me, he will keep my words: and my Father will love him, and we will come unto him, and make our abode with him.

John 14:23b

Yet the Lord will command his lovingkindness in the day-time, and in the night his song shall be with me, and my prayer unto the God of my life.

Psalm 42:8

PROSPERITY

THE Lord is my shepherd; I shall not want.

Psalm 23:1

And everyone that hath forsaken houses, or brethern, or sisters, or father, or mother, or wife, or children, or lands, for my name's sake, shall receive an hundredfold, and shall inherit everlasting life.

Matthew 19:29

I have been young, and now am old; yet have I not seen the righteous forsaken, nor his seed begging bread.

Psalm 37:25

The young lions do lack, and suffer hunger: but they that seek the Lord shall not want any good thing.

Psalm 34:10

Beloved, I wish above all things that thou mayest prosper and be in health, even as thy soul prospereth.

III John 2

The Lord shall command the blessing upon thee in thy storehouses, and in all that thou settest thine hand unto; and he shall bless thee in the land which the Lord thy God giveth thee.

Deuteronomy 28:8

The Lord shall open unto thee his good treasure, the heaven to give the rain unto thy land in his season, and to *bless all the work of thine hand: and thou shalt lend unto many nations, and thou shalt not borrow.*

Deuteronomy 28:12

Bring ye all the tithes into the storehouse, that there may be meat in mine house, and prove me now herewith, saith the Lord of hosts, if I will not open you the windows of heaven, and pour you out a blessing, that there shall not be room enough to receive it.

And I will rebuke the devourer for your sakes, and he shall not destroy the fruits of your ground; neither shall your vine cast her fruit before the time in the field, saith the Lord of hosts.

And all nations shall call you blessed: for you shall be a delightsome land, saith the Lord of hosts.

Malachi 3:10-12

Therefore take no thought, saying, What shall we eat? or, What shall we drink? or, Wherewithal shall we be clothed?

(For after all these things do the Gentiles seek:) for your heavenly Father knoweth that ye have need of all these things.

But seek ye first the kingdom of God, and his righteousness; and all these things shall be added unto you.

Matthew 6:31-33

Give, and it shall be given unto you; good measure, pressed down, and shaken together, and running over, shall men give into your bosom. For with the same measure that ye mete withal it shall be measured to you again.

Luke 6:38

And God is able to make all grace abound toward you; that ye, always having all sufficiency in all things, may abound to every good work:

II Corinthians 9:8

But my God shall supply all your need according to his riches in glory by Christ Jesus.

Philippians 4:19

A good man leaveth an inheritance to his children's children: and the wealth of the sinner is laid up for the just.

Proverbs 13:22

PRAYER

And it shall come to pass, that before they call, I will answer; and while they are yet speaking, I will hear.

Isaiah 65:24

But thou, when thou prayest, enter into thy closet, and when thou hast shut thy door, pray to thy Father which is in secret; and thy Father which seeth in secret shall reward thee openly.

Matthew 6:6

The Lord is nigh unto all them that call upon him, to all that call upon him in truth.

He will fulfil the desire of them that fear him; he also will hear their cry, and will save them.

Psalms 145:18,19

And whatsoever ye shall ask in my name, that will I do, that the Father may be glorified in the Son.

John 14:13

If ye abide in me, and my words abide in you, ye shall ask what ye will, and it shall be done unto you.

John 15:7

And in that day ye shall ask me nothing. Verily, verily, I say unto you, Whatsoever ye shall ask the Father in my name, he will give it you.

John 16:23

Jesus answered and said unto them, Verily I say unto you, if ye have faith, and doubt not, ye shall not only do this which is done to the fig tree, but also if ye shall say unto this mountain, Be thou removed, and be thou cast into the sea; it shall be done.

Matthew 21:21

Delight thyself also in the Lord; and he shall give thee the desires of thine heart.

Psalms 37:4

He shall call upon me, and I will answer him: I will be with him in trouble; I will deliver him and honour him.

Psalms 91:15

The Lord is far from the wicked: but he heareth the prayer of the righteous.

Proverbs 15:29

Call unto me, and I will answer thee, and shew thee great and mighty things, which thou knowest not.

Jeremiah 33:3

And whatsoever we ask, we receive of him, because we keep his commandments, and do those things that are pleasing in his sight.

I John 3:22

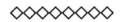

MERCY

I will be glad and rejoice in thy mercy: for thou hast considered my trouble; thou hast known my soul in adversities;

And hast not shut me up into the hand of the enemy: thou hast set my feet in a large room.

Psalm 31:7,8

Surely goodness and mercy shall follow me all the days of my life: and I will dwell in the house of the Lord forever.

Psalm 23:6

With the merciful thou wilt shew thyself merciful; with an upright man thou wilt shew thyself upright;

Psalm 18:25

I have been young, and now am old; yet have I not seen the righteous forsaken' nor his seed begging bread.

He is ever merciful, and lendeth; and his seed is blessed.

Psalm 37:25,26

The Lord is merciful and gracious, slow to anger, and plenteous in mercy.

Psalm 103:8

…and I will not cause mine anger to fall upon you: for I am merciful, saith the Lord, and I will not keep anger for ever.

Jeremiah 3:12b

Let us therefore come boldly to the throne of grace, that we may obtain mercy, and find grace to help in time of need.
Hebrews 4:16

Blessed are the merciful: for they shall obtain mercy.
Matthew 5:7

DELIVERANCE

For the law of the Spirit of life in Christ Jesus hath made me free from the law of sin and death.

Romans 8:2

But now being made free from sin, and become servants to God, ye have your fruit unto holiness, and the end everlasting life.

Romans 6:22

THE spirit of the Lord God is upon me; because the Lord has anointed me to preach good tidings unto the meek; he hath sent me to bind up the broken hearted, to proclaim liberty to the captives, and the opening of the prison to them that are bound;

Isaiah 61:1

The righteous cry, and the Lord heareth, and delivereth them out of all their troubles.

Psalm 34:17

Now the Lord is that Spirit: and where the Spirit of the Lord is, there is liberty.

II Corinthians 3:17

And these signs shall follow them that believe; In my name they shall cast out devils; they shall speak with new tongues;

Mark 16:17

Behold, I give unto you power to tread on serpents and scorpions, and over all the power of the enemy: and nothing shall by any means hurt you.

Luke 10:19

And they overcame him by the blood of the Lamb, and by the word of their testimony; and they loved not their lives unto the death.

Revelation 12:11

Ye are of God, little children, and have overcome them: because greater is he that is in you, than he that is in the world.

I John 4:4

VICTORY

Being confident of this very thing, that he which hath begun a good work in you will perform it until the day of Jesus Christ:

And this I pray, that your love may abound yet more and more in knowledge and in all judgment;

That ye may approve things that are excellent; that ye may be sincere and without offence till the day of Christ;

Philippians 1:6,9,10

Let us hold fast the profession of our faith without wavering; (for he is faithful that promised;)

Hebrews 10:23

But rejoice, inasmuch as ye are partakers of Christ's suffering; that, when his glory shall be revealed, ye may be glad also with exceeding joy.

I Peter 4:13

But we all, with open face beholding as in a glass the glory of the Lord, are changed into the same image from glory to glory, even as by the Spirit of the Lord.

II Corinthians 3:18

As for God, his way is perfect: the word of the Lord is tried: he is a buckler to all those that trust in him.

Psalm 18:30

Mine eye also shall see my desire on my enemies, and my ears shall hear my desire of the wicked that rise up against me.

The righteous shall flourish like the palm tree: he shall grow like a cedar in Lebanon.

Those that be planted in the house of the Lord shall flourish in the courts of our God.

They shall still bring forth fruit in old age; they shall be fat and flourishing;

To shew that the Lord is upright: he is my rock, and there is no unrighteousness in him.

Psalm 92:11-15

The Lord will perfect that which concerneth me: thy mercy, O Lord, endureth for ever: forsake not the works of thine own hands.

Psalm 138:8

PERSEVERANCE

Wait on the Lord: be of good courage, and he shall strengthen thine heart: wait, I say, on the Lord.

Psalm 27:14

I WAITED patiently for the Lord; and he inclined unto me, and heard my cry.

He brought me up also out of an horrible pit, out of the miry clay, and set my feet upon a rock, and established my goings.

And he hath put a new song in my mouth, even praise unto our God: many shall see it, and fear, and shall trust in the Lord.

Psalm 40:1-3

It is good that a man should both hope and quietly wait for the salvation of the Lord.

Lamentations 3:26

But they that wait upon the Lord shall renew their strength; they shall mount up with wings as eagles; they shall run, and not be weary; and they shall walk and not faint.

Isaiah 40:31

AND he spake a parable unto them to this end, that men ought always to pray, and not to faint;

Luke 18:1

But if we hope for that we see not, then do we with patience wait for it.

Romans 8:25

Cast not away therefore your confidence, which hath great recompence of reward.

For ye have need of patience, that, after ye have done the will of God, ye might receive the promise.

For yet a little while, and he that shall come will come, and will not tarry.

Now the just shall live by faith: but if any man draw back, my soul shall have no pleasure in him.

But we are not of them who draw back unto perdition; but of them that believe to the saving of the soul.

Hebrews 10:35-39

Knowing this, that the trying of your faith worketh patience.

But let patience have her perfect work, that ye may be perfect and entire, wanting nothing.

James 1:3,4

Be ye also patient; stablish your hearts: for the coming of the Lord draweth nigh.

James 5:8

LET US HEAR
THE CONCLUSION
OF THE WHOLE MATTER:
FEAR GOD, AND KEEP
HIS COMMANDMENTS:
FOR THIS IS THE WHOLE DUTY
OF MAN. FOR GOD
SHALL BRING EVERY WORK
INTO JUDGMENT,
WITH EVERY SECRET THING,
WHETHER IT BE GOOD, OR
WHETHER IT BE EVIL.

Ecclesiastes 12:13,14

◇◇◇◇◇◇◇◇

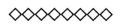

PART IV
JOURNAL

*Revelations
from the King*

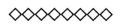

These pages are designated for your personal use as you learn and grow in the truths of God's word.

_____

_____

_____

_____

_____

_____

_____

_____

_____

_____

_____

_____

_____

SELAH.

About the Authors

Ruby Ridgill and Francine Morton were born into the Taylor family of twelve siblings in the small community of Alcolu, SC. They enjoyed a Godly home, stabilized by the constancy of prayer. Church attendance was never optional.

Although their spiritual enrichment was limited, neither of them realized how much so until well into their adult years. They were led in 1978 to visit Abundant Life Christian Centre in Margate, Florida where they learned that life is not "just life" for the here and now and the Kingdom is not a "mere illusion" for the hereafter. They learned that the Kingdom is here and now and in us. This revealed knowledge from God through Pastor Rick Thomas brought with it a conversion experience and transformation into a more meaningful and blessed life.

Their quest for truth about God and His Kingdom and for their place in the scheme of things led them into prayer. Here, they found themselves and their ministry of intercessory prayer. This, they learned, is where they fit into the plan of God.

Both Ruby and Francine are dedicated to the call to pray and are fully committed to a Kingdom life of daily intercessory prayer.

Printed in the United States
52777LVS00001B/16-18

9 781425 910785